The Mystery of
DEATH
&
DYING

The Mystery of DEATH & DYING

Initiation at the Moment of Death

Earlyne Chaney

SAMUEL WEISER, INC.
York Beach, Maine

First published in 1988 by
Samuel Weiser, Inc.
Box 612
York Beach, Maine 03910

Second printing, 1989

Library of Congress Cataloging in Publication Data:

Chancy, Earlyne.
    The mystery of death and dying/by Earlyne Chaney.
        p.   cm.
    Includes index.
    ISBN 0–87728–675–2
    1. Death.   2. Occultism.   I. Title.
BF1442.D43C45 1988
133.9'01'3 — dc19   87–34034
                                                        CIP

Text illustrations © 1988 Frances Paelian
Cover photography © 1988 Patricia Marshall

Typeset in 12 point Garamond
Printed in the United States of America

CONTENTS

To Locky

—Who chose to be a very special sister in this present incarnation.

—Who, from the very beginning til the very end, shared my laughter, my tears, my losses and my winnings, my valleys and my summits.

—Who was content to always walk one step behind, always supportive, always strengthening, always encouraging, and always there.

There is a secret to the art of dying. The soul faces the timeless moment of initiation into life's most secret and sacred mystery. The light seeker will enter paradise. The average soul will enter the high astral. The dark soul will walk the lonesome valley of the judgment. But all will eventually evolve toward the heart of God.

PREFACE

EVER SINCE THE human race experienced the great Fall—the descent of the soul into the field of matter—we have probed the mystery of death. Ever since the great Lord God commanded, saying, "Of every tree of the garden thou mayest freely eat—but of the tree of the knowledge of good and evil thou shalt not eat, for in the day thou eatest thereof thou shalt surely die," we have pondered the mystery of the inevitable destiny of the soul, the celestial sentence of death which makes us mortal. Through the ages we have tried to lift the veil that separates our matter world from the spirit world—to fathom the enigma of the inexorable transition.

It would be difficult to determine when the present current of new age awakening actually occurred, when acceptance of life after death actually came to be part of our rational thinking. Was it in the tiny cottage of the Fox sisters in Hydesville, New York, around 1850, when mysterious raps on the headboard of their bed gave birth to the singular sect of controversial discord called Spiritualism? Was it the apparitions of the Blessed Virgin as she appeared in numerous places all over the world, asking people to reconcile their differences, to pray, to do penance? What suddenly—or gradually—made the theory of life after death, psychism, reincarnation, regression—indeed, death itself—so acceptable, "talkable," even respectable? It couldn't have happened at any one moment in time. Like a slow-breaking dawn, it has filtered into our consciousness and, again like dawn, has infused darkness with light.

Today, death and all its mysteries can be openly discussed. Suddenly those who do *not* believe in life after death are the erratic ones. And now a mystic can begin to discuss the dying process, for not only is death a timely subject, but there is an art to doing it—a right way to die just as there is a right way to live.

My only claim to authority is a lifetime of questing—and, through that questing, catching a glimpse of eternal verities beyond the mists of time and space that bind our world of matter. I think from the first moment I drew the breath of life, my consciousness was pervaded by thoughts of death—not the proverbial fear of death and dying, but rather the opposite—a longing to pierce the mystery, to understand what happens to people when they die, what of the soul, what of heaven and hell, and what did it really mean to be saved.

In my book *Remembering—The Autobiography of a Mystic*,* I share the vivid experience of losing someone I loved—a World War II pilot. Following his death, I turned from a career as a film actress to enter the world of mysticism on a quest to reach my beloved on the other side of the veil. And reach him I did. But the quest brought far

_____

Remembering—The Autobiography of a Mystic (Upland, CA: Astara, 1974).

more than a revelation of life after death. It brought a sudden spiritual illumination, and turned me toward a lifetime of teaching, healing, writing and sharing the illimitable concepts which poured into my consciousness from a great Master Teacher dwelling on the other side.

I remember as a child, one day a neighbor called to my mother from across the street, "Mae, old man Cox died last night from a heart attack." And my mother replied, "Good! That old reprobate! He got just what he deserved." None of my playmates even paused, but I stood stock still, pondering. Then ran away to sit alone, questioning my unseen Teacher. Death must be God's greatest punishment! But because the silent voice assured me otherwise — well, perhaps that small incident helped to trigger my long, unending quest to unravel the mystery of death and dying.

It was this Master's presence that inspired me to write about death and teach the science of dying to those attending my seminars. It was he who first taught me that death need not be an event to be feared or dreaded. It is actually a type of initiation — a testing time, a judgment time, a time when the soul meets the greatest challenge of its entire incarnation and decides upon what plane it may best fulfill its destiny.

It was only after I had completely absorbed these concepts that I was able to disseminate them. The teachings presented here are not mine. They have been filtered through my mind as I, acting as amanuensis, wrote them down that you might make them an important part of your faith. "Teach them," said Kut-Hu-Mi, "to look to death as life's greatest challenge, life's greatest test, life's greatest adventure, the time of the true initiation." The great Teacher was most anxious that those who believe in life after death realize that the actual process of death, itself, should be understood.

"There is an art to dying," he frequently reminded me. "Teach the light seekers the science of dying. Point them toward the secrets. Knowing how to die is as important as knowing how to live. Indeed, once one understands the mystery of death and dying, the greater is the assurance that a worthy and significant life will be lived; not simply a good life, but an incarnation of seeking the baptism of Holy Spirit, a life of active prayer, a life of meditating to activate the dormant power of kundalini.

"Once you understand that these spiritual forces will become active during death, bringing the soul a final opportunity for illumination, then the more earnestly will you seek these unfoldments during life — resulting in a life of light seeking. Certainly you will avoid building a karmic record of negative thought patterns once it is understood that these thoughtforms become active as 'dwellers on the threshold' during the death journey called the Bardo."

My Teacher was not interested in *proving* life after death; he wanted to help enlighten those who already believe. He pointed out that we can only attain the Godhead by degrees, and we will arrive at various spiritual plateaus along the way as follows:

1) First, you slowly become aware that there is life after death.

2) Second, you will learn there is a right way to die.

3) Third, you must understand the importance of seeking the baptism of Holy Spirit and learn to awaken kundalini power during both life and death.

4) Next, you must know that the third step — the baptism of Holy Spirit — is actually the first step, because only via

such a baptism does the soul become immortal, attaining its liberation from the wheel of rebirth.

The Master Kut-Hu-Mi is forever indicating that his teachings are only reflections of what the great Lord Jesus would have him teach. He prefaces most of his teachings by the words, "The Great Lord Jesus would have me say _____"; then he proceeds with remarkable teachings, astonishing answers to many questions, and ancient wisdom straight from the Mystery Schools of antiquity.

It is with joy I release this information, knowing full well it is not my own. It is an ingathering of a great deal of wisdom concerning life, death, rebirth, the soul, the spirit — and the great God who made us all. It points us toward the hidden way across the threshold into the waiting arms of a Savior more meaningful than the traditional Savior of our Christianized concept. The Christ is indeed the Savior of all souls, not simply those of Christianity. He waits to "save" us from ever needing to return to Earth life again. This Christ is not only Jesus — but Buddha, Mohammed, Siva, Krishna, Osiris, Moses — all the great ones of the light. This Christ is the force behind all avatars, all messiahs, all wayshowers.

So I write without hesitation: the Christ would have me say, "_there is an art to dying_." May these words become guidelines to point us toward prayer and deep soul meditation, bringing the grace of Holy Spirit which fills the soul with the divine essence of God, and, penetrating the very heart of every seeker, guide us to everlasting salvation.

Chapter One

THE AKASHIC RECORD

GOD, THE MACROCOSM, the cosmic atom, reflects in the microcosm, the human atom. Light seekers are familiar with the Hermetic axiom: "As it is above, so is it below." We are also familiar with the biblical scripture which reminds us that the spirit is made in the image of our Father/Mother God. We might say that human beings are microcosmic atoms on and in the body of the cosmic macrocosmic God. We are gods in embryo. We are gods in the making. (See figure 1 on page 2.)

Earth is surrounded by its own auric forcefields. We tend to think that Earth has its boundaries at the periphery, the circumference, of the planet itself. But this is not so. Its ultimate boundary extends into the atmosphere, into immeasurable space, and includes the spheres of life that we experience after the death of our physical form. Thus the ultimate measurement of true Earth includes the astral, mental, causal and all the encompassing spiritual planes. (See figure 2 on page 4.)

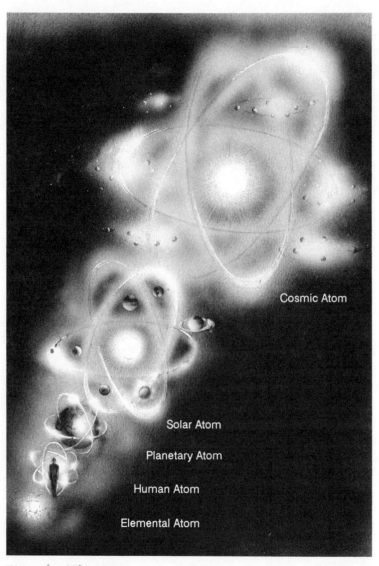

Figure 1. The Hermetic Law: As it is above, so it is below.

As Earth is surrounded by its invisible forcefields—as an egg holds a central yolk—so are we surrounded by our invisible auric forcefield. We have not one body, but seven. For want of a better terminology, we call the surrounding sheaths _bodies_—the etheric, astral, mental, causal, celestial. They are actually seven mystical principles enclosed and interblended within our auric forcefield. As above, so below. As it is with the planet, so is it with humanity.

Each vesture, sheath or body is composed of its own harmonious atomic structure, each vibrating at its own frequency and each surrounded by a forcefield of its own substance, just as our physical form is encompassed by our own physical aura.

No illustration on a flat three dimensional surface can embody the teaching. It can only point toward reality. Let us, however, imagine a sponge—a sponge of many colors. Let us say that the center of the sponge is brown, and around that small brown center is a circle of red, with some of the red interpenetrating the brown. And around the red circle is one of green, and another of blue, and another of yellow—until the sponge has seven circles of color, with each of the fields of color interpenetrating the others, yet each held in its own radius by its individual frequency.

Now let us immerse this variegated sponge in a glass bowl of water, and call the water _pranic life force_. We cannot see the water-prana that interpenetrates every particle of the vari-colored sponge, but we know that it is so interpenetrated.

We can relate this vari-colored sponge to the dense physical body and its surrounding forcefields. The brown center would represent our dense physical form. The circle around it is the astral form, and the other circles are our

Figure 2. Earth is surrounded by astral, mental, causal and celestial spheres.

various other "bodies." Each of these colors penetrates the dense physical form, and the entire physical form-sponge is immersed in a sea of pranic life force, or ether.

Let us say that a part of the form-sponge is suddenly dry and dead—cut off from the surrounding pranic life force. Particularly we are referring to the brown center, the dense physical form in the center of the sponge. Without being interpenetrated by the pranic life force, the center of the sponge is dead. Only when it is immersed in the bowl of pranic life force does it manifest life, mind, consciousness and total being. When the life force is withdrawn, it dies.

Now let us imagine that the walls of the glass bowl are porous; they are infinitely fine. And then let us immerse this glass bowl with its pranic life force containing the sponge-form in an immeasureable tank of energized water, or pranic life force of high voltage. There we have a vision of our total being immersed in a sea of divine life forces. The bowl and the immersed sponge-form represent you and your total auric forcefield, and it is porous and sensitive to the inpouring, surrounding sea of Akashic ethers about it.

Now let us speak of our bodies as being physical, etheric, astral, mental, intuitional, monadic, and celestial. For our purposes in this book, we shall relate principally to the physical, etheric, astral and mental. The physical body manifests two aspects:

The dense physical—composed of the solids, liquids, and gases that doctors and anatomical scientists recognize;

The etheric double—the counterpart of the dense physical body, which is composed of four higher physical ethers— and of which medical science is unaware.

We shall not at this particular writing delve into the composition of these four physical ethers. Ancient wisdom calls them the light, pranic, Akashic, and mental reflecting ethers. To research them is a complete teaching in itself.[1] For our present research, we shall simply call them the four higher physical plane ethers, meaning they are beyond our present human perception.

The astral body is composed of two aspects also: *the Kama Rupa*—the body of lower desires; and *the astral body*—the body of higher desires.

The mental body is also composed of two aspects: *the lower mental body*—which registers concrete thoughts, or the thoughts of our everydayness, our waking conscious mind; and *the higher mental or causal body*—which registers abstract thought, or the thoughts of the superconscious mind.

Now let us refer to the force centers in the body, which are called *chakras*. In all arcane records, constant reference is made to *force centers* in both the microcosmic human being and the macrocosmic Being. The Sanskrit writers called them chakras, and since there seems to be no better English derivative to describe them, we shall also refer to them as chakras. The word means *a wheel of energy*, or a *vortex of power*. Chakras are located at strategic points along the spine and in the brain, superimposing the major endocrine glands of our physical form. The centers closely resemble wheels in motion. Pouring out from the center of the wheel, or "hub," are streams of radiation, rays of energy and power, which, seen clairvoyantly,

---

[1]See, for example, *The Book of Life*, a series of degree teachings which have been channeled through Earlyne Chaney, available only to members of Astara. For more information, write Astara, PO Box 5003, Upland, CA 91786

appear to resemble the whirling spokes of a wheel. The chakras also resemble flowers. The lines of radiation often take the form and symmetry of flower petals.

There are seven major chakras. It is through these whirling vortices that etheric pranic life force is indrawn and, entering the physical glands, is distributed into the bloodstream. The chakras are described as the root chakra (1), navel (2), solar plexus (3), heart (4), throat (5), brow (6), and crown (7).

Root chakra: Superimposes the genital organs and glands at the base of the spinal column. It resembles an unfolded flower with four large petals. Our largest center of subconsciousness is located in the root chakra, sometimes called "the root brain." Also coiled there is _kundalini_, the center of our potential divinity, about which we shall talk later.

Navel chakra: Superimposes the prostatic area in the male and the uterus in the female, located in the center of the body about two inches below the navel. This chakra radiates six streams of power. It is extremely active, since it is through this center that much prana is indrawn into the etheric body. We would appear to absorb most of our pranic vitality and oxygen through the lungs, but this is not true. Much is indrawn through this navel chakra, which also embraces the spleen. The spleen is the manufacturer of blood cells, thus the inpouring prana and new blood cells are carried by our bloodstream throughout the physical form, distributing life force. A biblical axiom succinctly posits that "the life is in the blood." Pranic life force, indrawn through the navel-splenic chakra and distributed through the body via the bloodstream, rises out of the navel chakra.

Solar plexus chakra: Superimposes the solar plexus area—
the adrenal/pancreas glands and liver. At our present state
of evolution, this is probably the most sensitive of all the
chakras. It is the point of vital contact between the astral
and physical bodies. Here is found the astral or "abdominal brain," the center of feelings and emotions. It is
undoubtedly the most active of all the chakras, in that we
are presently governed principally by emotions. That
which we desire at any given moment becomes the principal thrust of our thought power. We do not always exhibit
good judgment in relation to our desires. Thus a major
portion of time, most people are ruled by the abdominal
brain—by the desire emotions rather than will or logic.

These three lower centers—the root, navel, and solar
plexus chakras—compose the lower self, or carnal being.
From these centers flow the life force of selfishness, greed,
lust and hate, empowered by our thoughts, our mental
force. Some souls never rise in consciousness above these
animalistic qualities. The lower carnal self dominates the
life until, through spiritual seeking, meditation, or prayer,
the dynamic but partially dormant force of kundalini in
the root chakra becomes active. Awakening and ascension
of the kundalini through the spinal cord marks a transformation in the soul, and points the soul Godward.

Heart chakra: Superimposes the thymus gland between
the shoulder blades and extends to embrace the heart center. The heart is the midway point between the three lower
and the three higher chakras. This chakra ultimately
becomes the seat of love and compassion, which, in the
majority, is not as developed as the emotional center.
Although love is a tremendous force in our lives, at our

present evolutionary status desire-love dominates more of our thoughts and actions than does our heart-love.

Throat chakra: Superimposes the thyroid gland in the throat and extends to embrace the medulla oblongata. The medulla oblongata, located in the base of the brain, is a tremendous seat of spiritual vitality and is of supreme spiritual significance. It is in the heart and throat chakras that the consciousness of the seeker of light usually focuses at our present evolutionary level. The heart is the center of compassion and the throat that of creativity. The seeker predominantly expresses these two qualities.

Brow chakra: Superimposes the pituitary gland. The brow-pituitary center is the seat of our renowned sixth sense, from which flows the expression of extrasensory perception. It is the sense-center of higher abstract aspiration, the visionary quality, the seat of intuition. This sixth sense of clairsentient perception, which we all possess but which we don't always express, is becoming increasingly active. At the present, the female expresses this intuitive perception more frequently than the male—probably because the male is oriented toward the outer or material world. The female, being the childbearer, concentrates much of her attention upon the child, the love of which arouses the pituitary center, whereas the male, of necessity, focuses upon the material world, the better to supply those he loves with what is necessary for survival—food, roof, etc.

Crown chakra: Superimposes the pineal gland and radiates upward and outward to encompass the entire crown of the head. Containing innumerable petals—or radiating streams of pranic energy—this chakra is frequently called

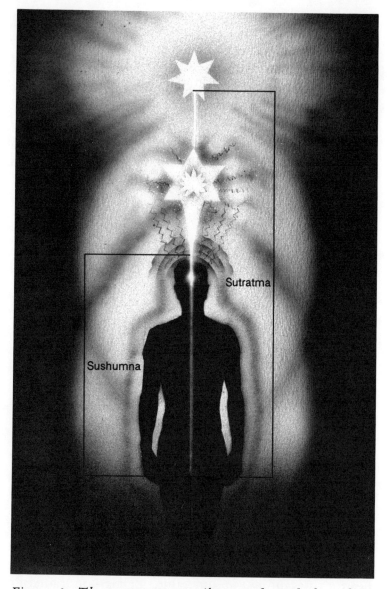

Figure 3. The sutratma, or silver cord, and the etheric spinal cord, which is called the sushumna.

the thousand petaled lotus. The crown chakra, at present, lies like an etheric skull-cap over the top of the head. Ultimately, as it attains its mature function, it will extend upward to radiate as a light around the head.

This seventh center is sometimes called the _Brahmaranda_. Its aureole, once activated, rises in magnificent splendor to unite with the Oversoul. Its colors can only be described as white light, changing intermittently from the soft glow of moonlight to the dazzling brilliance of blinding sunlight. As these rays flow upward, they resemble the radiating forces of an aurora borealis, exhibiting incredible flashes of incomparable colors. It is the outflow of these radiant rays that manifests as the halo around the head of god-beings, such as Jesus, Mary, Buddha, Krishna. The halo signifies that the crown chakra has attained its ultimate glory and that kundalini is fully awakened and ascended.

We must now speak of the sutratma, the silver cord of biblical renown, linking together the three aspects of the human being — the physical, soul and spirit. The sutratmic silver cord extends from the base of the spine (the root chakra) to the monad, which we symbolize by the seven-pointed star above the head. (See figure 3.) In the physical form, from the top of the head to the base of the spine, it is called the _sushumna_ (shoo-_shoom_-na). In the ancient wisdom teachings, sushumna and sutratma are extensions of each other — like Main Street merging into Broadway. The cord changes in vibration as it departs the top of the head to become a living stream of light to connect with the monad above the head.

The sutratma, or soul thread, emanates from the heart of the monad. It projects downward to the causal

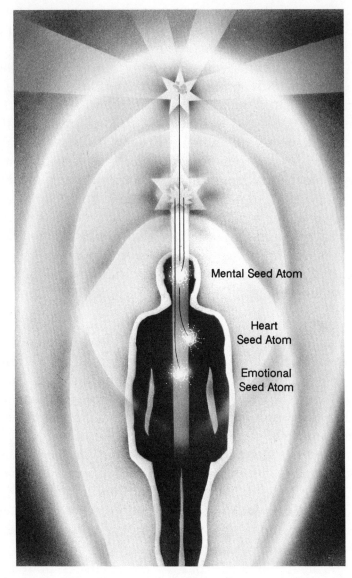

Mental Seed Atom

Heart
Seed Atom

Emotional
Seed Atom

Figure 4. The three cords and the three seed atoms.

plane, where a soul is created. The soul, in turn, projects the cord down into the dense world of matter where it becomes embodied in the personality.

Along the silver cord are attached _the three permanent seed atoms_. These three seed atoms are of major importance in life and in death. They have a significance in learning about death. We call them _permanent_ because they are just that. They became an innate part of you when you first manifested as an individualized soul in the human kingdom. They come with you each time you are born again for a new incarnation, and they depart with you each time you die. They are your soul's _Book of Life_, or your _Book of Judgment_, containing your personal Akashic Record. They embody within themselves the seed pattern of the individual soul, just as an acorn ensouls within itself all that will become the oak tree. Everything you have done, said or thought is recorded in the seed atoms of your own being. These three seed atoms are strung like magnificent jewels along this shining river of light, the sutratma. (See figure 4.) One is called the _emotional_, or _astral, seed atom_, another the _mental seed atom_, and a third the _heart seed atom_.

The Emotional Seed Atom

The emotional seed atom, shown in figure 5 on page 14, is located in the solar plexus in the great apex of the liver. It has stamped upon it all the qualities of the emotions ever experienced by your soul. It ensouls all the inherent weaknesses and strengths of character developed by your soul as far as your desires and emotions are concerned.

Figure 5. The emotional cord and the emotional seed atom. The emotional cord extends between the soul-lotus (or Oversoul) and the solar plexus region.

Let's consider a typical "weakness." Let's say that John Smith becomes an alcoholic. It's not surprising, the neighbors say, since his father had the same problem. John just "inherited" the weakness from his father. Not so. He brought his own alcoholic tendencies with him at birth, buried as a characteristic deep in the astral seed atom. A soul will often choose parents, or they are chosen for him, because they have harmonious karma. But no soul "inherits" a character weakness. Think of the many children with alcoholic fathers who did _not_ become alcoholic.

Each soul must meet and either surrender to or overcome residual seed karma. John became an alcoholic because, in his past life, he surrendered to an excessive desire for alcohol and did not overcome that desire. He brought the tendency toward his craving with him into this new incarnation. He chose his particular father as a parent because his similar soul characteristic tendency created a harmonious vibratory bondage. It was easy to link with the frequency wavelength of his father's seed atom and come into rebirth. This new life offered the opportunity to overcome the inherent seed atom tendency. Many surrender again to the craving, but many overcome it.

This seed atom, containing the record of your past desires, also reflects your present emotional life. It perpetually pours atomic particles into the bloodstream, carrying their influence on into the glandular system. The point to be remembered is that although it is the sum total of all your emotional qualities and characteristics, nevertheless it can be changed in quality at any moment by your efforts for you can totally dissipate all remaining negative qualities. Such would be instant conversion—being "saved by grace." The astral seed atom, then, concerns the present and the future of the person, the soul. The individual can instantly decide to give up alcohol — and the seed atom will reflect this positive soul quality.

The solar plexus chakra, frequently called the abdominal brain because it is the seat of the emotional seed atom, is a major reason why human beings are presently so dominated by desires. Flowing out of this atom into the bloodstream are the infinitesimal "picture images" of all of your emotional weaknesses. But, again, be aware that you are in complete control of this center. Awareness of the presence of this atom, and its influence in your daily life, changes the outflow of the picture images at any time for you can change the quality of the atomic particles. You can elevate your desire from the carnal to the spiritual in "the twinkling of an eye." You can begin to desire that which is of more spiritual benefit in your life. This atom changes daily, reflecting every momentary emotional change. If you are fairly stable emotionally, the atom will reflect the peaceful aura of balance, harmony, kindness — the colors, the sounds of love essence. But if you are subject to anger, fear, jealousy, hate, lust, the auric pattern of the seed atom will reflect the churning essences of these emotional upheavals.

Once a seeker becomes aware of this desire atom, you will realize how much attention is centered upon the desire for "things" of Earth. Such an awareness usually shifts the focus to that which is more important. It is natural to desire that which is good of this earthly realm, but it is not wise to allow such desires to dominate one's life. Being aware that the negative picture images flow constantly into the bloodstream, dominating your life, aids in placing emphasis upon that which should have priority.

It is not negative or "evil" to desire a diamond ring, or to possess it if you do not allow the desire for _it_ to possess _you_. If you are in full control of what is the supreme desire in your life, you can benefit by possessing the wealth of the world — as long as you do not allow it to control you. Seldom, however, is material wealth used for the betterment of humankind. Rather, it usually is used toward the glamor of a purposeless lifestyle — thus becoming a spiritual "curse" and not a blessing.

So be aware of what flows out of that emotional seed atom. Shift the emphasis of your desires away from things of Earth to the treasures of heaven. Remember the biblical admonition about the treasures of Earth. "Lay not up for yourselves treasures on Earth, where moth and rust corrupt, and where thieves break through and steal. But lay up for yourselves treasures in Heaven, where neither moth nor rust corrupt and where thieves do not break through nor steal: For where your treasure is, there will your heart be also" (Matthew 6:19–21).[2]

The point is that once you are aware of this emotional seed atom and its influence, do not allow it to further dominate your life. This does not imply that we should relinquish all aims and purposes here on Earth and center attention entirely upon the spiritual. We were meant _also_ to have goals during an incarnation, and to develop skills and talents. Every soul should leave the world a better place for having been here. When you desire a better home here on Earth, give equal time to desiring a beautiful home Overthere, which can only be attained by purified emotions, deeds and thoughts.

---

[2]This and all subsequent biblical citations are from the King James Version of the Bible.

Figure 6. The consciousness cord and the mental seed atom. This cord extends between the seat of the supercon-scious mind in the Oversoul to the mental seed atom, located in the pineal gland in the brain.

The Mental Seed Atom

The mental seed atom is located in the pineal gland in the brain. This seed atom is, again, a record of all you have *thought* in all the eons past, since you became an individualized soul in the human kingdom. (See figure 6.)

This atom contains the cosmic record of your thought vibrations and patterns. Its colors and frequencies fluctuate according to the voltage of your thoughts. Like mercury rising and falling in a thermometer, it registers your high and low thought essence. When your thoughts are pervaded by an undercurrent of love, the mental seed atom radiates wavelengths of high voltage, attracting white light thoughtwaves from higher planes and higher minds. When selfishness, cunning and carnality pervade the consciousness, the mercury of the atom drops, the colors dim, the frequency diminishes. Knowledge of this atom behooves you to saturate every action with love thoughts, and love energy. It is especially important that the mental seed atom register a love energy at the moment of death.

This seed atom can also be changed at any moment. "Be ye transformed by the renewing of your mind" (Romans 12:2). At any moment, you can "renew" or change your mind. You can change the quality of the picture images emerging from the pineal seed atom into the bloodstream. Your thoughts are under your complete domination, your willpower. When you become aware of the mental seed atom and its influence in your life, you begin to "watch" your thoughts, to be aware there are picture images flowing constantly into the bloodstream, reflecting the quality of your thoughtforce at each passing moment.

The auric forcefield around you is in a state of flux, responding to the caliber of your thoughts. Becoming aware that this seed atom is recording your entire thought-life, you will begin to combine it with your emotions, and elevate your desires to that which is more permanent in your destiny: seeking the treasures of heaven. You will think kindness, purity, service. You will be aware that if you desire a beautiful home Overthere, you must express a beautiful thoughtforce during Earth life — because the substance of that thoughtforce is the substance of which your home is composed Overthere. The souls who focus their attention upon greed, money, self aggrandizement, or power over others can only inherit a hovel on the lower planes because that world is a thought world.

This mental seed atom bears a record of all the inherited and innate qualities of the mind. It registers the total mind power developed by the soul during the ages of its evolutionary progress. It is also an atom of both present and future in that you can create changes in it immediately by changing your mind. It is today what you have made of it in past incarnations. It is particularly representative of the quality of thoughts you expressed in your last four incarnations. Your present mind level could be influenced especially by your last incarnation. Even so, it can be endowed with greater powers *now* to affect both the immediate present and the future. It is altogether different concerning the seed atom in the heart.

The Heart Seed Atom

This is the atom that contains the record of your total past, including the physical, emotional and mental aspects.

Whereas the astral and mental seed atoms contain only the *qualities* of the emotions and the mind, the heart seed atom contains a complete electronic visual recording of everything that has ever happened to the soul throughout its existence. Whereas the astral and the mental seed atoms release into the bloodstream the qualities of the emotions and the mind, the physical heart seed atom releases actual atomic picture images of the past. (See figure 7 on page 22.)

To quote again a biblical scripture, "As a man thinketh in his heart, so is he" (Proverbs 23:7). This is the seed atom that records every emotion, every thought, every action, every deed—everything you ever think, say or do. It has created, and is creating, a motion picture record of the total YOU and your present incarnation—so that, if you could sit at the end of the day and view it, you would see not only a complete motion picture drama of all that you did during the day, but all that you thought, all that you felt, all that you expressed mentally, physically and emotionally. All is recorded there in its action, in its karmic action.

The question is often asked, "Are we puppets of fate and karmic destiny, or are we free souls with the power to choose our own fate and destiny?" The enigma has long perplexed the seeker. The answer is found in the knowledge of these three seed atoms. The heart seed atom, containing its perpetual record of your past, ties you to your karmic destiny, while the mental and astral seed atoms, containing the characteristic powers or weaknesses, enable you to control your future, your own destiny. Thus you have two seed atoms subject to your free will and a destiny of your own choosing—and you have one seed

Figure 7. The life cord and the heart seed atom. The fears, guilts and phobias, buried in the subconscious, are also recorded in the heart seed atom as karma. These karmic picture images, carried into the brain cells via the bloodstream, continually release electronic impulses which strike the "tape" of mental reflecting ether in the subconscious area. The subconscious mind force carries the fears into the waking conscious, which drifts from "memory" to "memory." Thus we are victims of our karma, and the superconscious cannot gain prominence until the heart seed atom is cleared.

atom securely holding you to your karmic past destiny and "fate."

Can you overcome the karma of the past in the heart seed atom? Indeed so, if you so choose. But it requires spiritual prowess beyond the evolution of most people. You would have to live at the summit of your purity if you are to offset the influence of the picture images of past karma emptying vibratory essences into the bloodstream. This is what the Master meant when we were admonished to overcome evil with good. You thereby nullify the karmic effect of the heart seed atom upon the glandular system. The dark karma of the past must be so offset by the powerful charges of the light of the present _good_ pouring from the mental-astral atoms that past karma of the heart atom cannot take root in the glands and will lose its power to be negatively effective.

The infinitesimal picture images flowing from the heart atom into the bloodstream strike the endocrine glands. The glands respond by withholding hormones necessary for perfect physical expression, or they pour out balanced hormonic substances to create a perfected physical life. The choice depends upon the karma in the images reeling out of the heart seed atom.

The heart seed atom has an effect on the physical being, in that if in past lives or in the present, you have committed deeds to warrant a karmic retribution, at a certain point in your life the karmic heart seed images will begin flowing into the bloodstream, creating physical disabilities. Perhaps you will experience weakened eyes, problems of hearing, the distress of arthritis, or some other illness that will prevent, delay, or restrict the mission you hoped to complete during your Earth sojourn. Again, this karma can be overcome, but it requires almost transcendental effort. You must *constantly* guard your thoughts and perform at the peak of your spiritual awareness at all times. This is a major challenge and few can totally measure up to it. Daily prayer is a certain means of purifying the heart atom, of dissipating past records, and of healing both the body and the soul.

Of course, an illness or difficulty *could* be caused by present actions—such as lifestyle, diet, etc. The karmic illness usually refers to a major disease that persistently prevents one from pursuing long-sought goals.

We need to consider another biblical quotation: "The Lord is long-suffering and of great mercy, forgiving iniquity and transgression, and by no means clearing the guilty, visiting the iniquity of the fathers upon the children unto the third and fourth generation" (Numbers 14:18).

What could this possibly mean? Could it be that you are responsible for the sins, mistakes and karma of your father, your grandfather, and on back to the fourth generation? This would certainly manifest a most cruel and unjust God. It would appear that the original teaching has been lost, or changed by copyists and interpreters of the scriptures. It would seem to refer to your own last four incarnations. Ancient wisdom makes you solely responsible for the karma of your incarnations, the last four of which may still dominate you in this particular life.

To harmonize with the wisdom teachings, the scripture should read that the karma of the "father" is visited upon the "child" unto the fourth *incarnation*, not generation. The mistakes you made in the last four incarnations may be visited upon you in the form of karma flowing out of the heart seed atom in the present incarnation. Thus what you "fathered," or created, in your last incarnation may be the source ("parent") of your karma today. You are a *child* of that parent today. You have inherited from *that* parent — the you of the past, not your physical parents — all of your characteristics, weaknesses and strengths.

If your mother has weak eyes and you have "inherited" weak eyes, you did not inherit them from her. You inherited them from the karmic picture images in your heart seed atom. In the genes she gave you, she may have given to your physical form the potential for weak eyes, but you would develop them only if you deserved them — only if you, too, possessed the potential in the karma of your heart seed atom.

When the seed of a soul is planted in the womb of the mother-to-be, there is first built an etheric pattern in the matrix of the womb, established by the domination of the heart seed atom, and bearing your karmic record. The pattern of your etheric body is structured according to your past karma. As we have already explained, the etheric body is composed of the four higher physical ethers.

The etheric form is diffused throughout the physical body. These four physical ethers are called "space plasma." If the etheric double could be separated from the physical body intact, and studied, it would be found to be a perfect duplicate of the physical form, but having no mind — rather like the infamous zombie, full of life force but without mind force. It is a highly complex structure, a generator of tremendous electromagnetic power, a battery for the physical form. Without the etheric form and its prana, your physical form is dead as without the battery, your car is dead. The battery is not your car, nor is prana your physical form.

When the spirit leaves the body at the time of death, it leaves behind both the shell of the physical form and its etheric double. The two become slightly detached and disintegrate together. It requires the two of them, operating as a unit, to express life. The physical form without the vital etheric form interpenetrating it is only an empty shell and possesses no vital life.

During the process of gestation, the infant form is building in the matrix of the womb. The cells of the new-forming physical body adhere to the atoms of the etheric double, which forms the archetypical pattern for the dense physical form—an etheric "scaffolding"—structured and governed by the influence of karmic images in the heart seed atom of the incoming soul. The etheric is built first, lying in the matrix of the womb of the mother-to-be.

The atoms of this etheric double form the pattern, or matrix, upon which the new physical form is to be molded. The etheric double, the pranic body, takes the shape that destiny dictates for this particular incarnation, based upon past karma, and flows out of the heart seed atom.

Thus the old personality, that which you were in your last incarnations, is the parent of the present. According to the way you molded the etheric form in your last four incarnations, so it comes forth in this new incarnation. It is in this sense that "the sins of the father are visited upon the child even unto the fourth generation." So the sins—or karma—of the last four personalities, but particularly the last one, are impregnated within the atoms of the etheric double and will come forward into the new etheric double of the present personality. The "very hairs of your head are numbered," according to the thoughts and actions of your past record. The etheric body is the reflection of the soul at its lowest spiritual manifestation.

Think again of the sponge. It has the dense physical form at its center, manifesting as a spot of brown. It contains also this etheric double, the pattern of your past. The physical form, molded upon the pattern of the etheric, expresses the soul's very lowest potential. We are therefore somehow responsible for the forms we inherit in each new incarnation. The body of our new personality will relate to our destiny.

We can overcome the karma pouring out of the heart seed atom if we become *aware* and live at our very highest and best. But there are some karmic patterns that cannot be dispelled. Sometimes a soul, before incarnating again, chooses to take a karmic burden upon itself. The celestial guardian will make the soul aware that accepting such a burden can accelerate certain opportunities needed by the soul for its progression. For example, a soul may choose one lifetime of total blindness or lameness rather than four of semi-affliction.

The soul will assume this dire aspect of karma to dissipate the record forever. This kind of accepted karma can rarely be overcome or healed. So there is the answer to the query: "Are we free souls or victims of a fate already planned?" To repeat, through two seed atoms you are free and can choose your destiny. But simultaneously, you are held by one infinitesimal seed atom to your past—your own misdeeds, your own weaknesses.

Our karmic past relates to the timeless query: "Which came first—the chicken or the egg?" The answer is that the seed always must precede the birth. Therefore the egg preceded the chicken. The egg had its beginning as a seed in the long-ago past, and has been referred to as the great cosmic egg. Just so, the seeds of karma in the heart atom had their first beginning in the long-ago past of evolution. We are now well on our way to attaining a lifetime when the seed atom in the heart will exude only excellence into the bloodstream. The images released to influence the glands will be a constant stream of purified, powerfully charged particles of life, love and divine energy.

Chapter Two

DEATH AND THE DIVINE FIRE

LET'S SPEAK NOW of *kundalini*. The kundalini has been termed both "the divine fire in man," and "the fiery furnace." It is a fragmentary spark of the divine fire. Simultaneously, it is a fiery furnace to the unskilled neophyte who attempts to play with fire with no knowledge of potential purification. Kundalini is a dynamic coil of psycho-spiritual power lying partially dormant at the base of the spine in the root chakra, coiled like a serpent in an area called the *kanda*. By mystics and initiates of the Mystery Schools it was known as "the serpent fire."

Subject to the influence of the sympathetic nervous system, it produces the formation of the sperm in the male and the ovum in the female, resulting in the ever-recurring cycle of the creative sexual urge. In the average individual, the activity of kundalini seldom deviates from this automatic function. A small portion rises through sushumna (the soul thread transpiercing the spinal cord) to stimulate creative aspiration in the brain-mind centers in the artist,

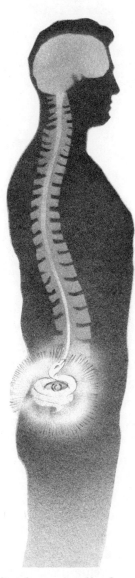

Figure 8. Kundalini lies partially dormant in the root chakra in the average individual.

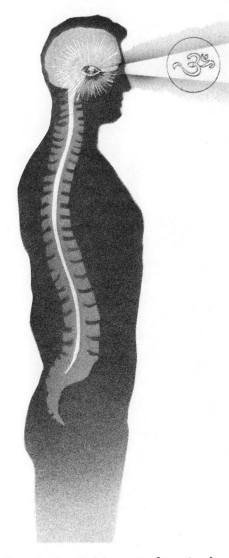

Figure 9. In mystics, initiates and yogis, kundalini occasionally rises up the spine, strikes all the chakras and opens the third eye.

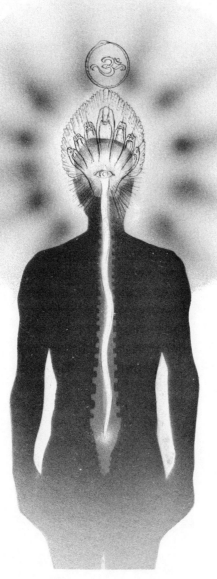

Figure 10. In the ascended Master, kundalini remains elevated with the third eye active, resulting in full use of cosmic awareness.

the writer, the scientist, the creative thinker. Figure 8 on page 30 depicts kundalini in the average person.

But in the light seeker, the mystic, the yogi—those who meditate, pray, study the mysteries, or practice the presence of love toward all humankind—the embers of the kundalini stir into an active fire—a cosmic fire.

Figure 9 (on page 31) depicts kundalini active and the third eye opened. Mystics, yogis and initiates occasionally, through prayer, meditation or service, arouse the kundalini power and send it spiraling upward through the spinal column, to strike the pineal-pituitary glands in the brain, resulting in momentary illumination. These momentary and usually infrequent stirrings bring flashes of intuitive perception, clairvoyant visions, premonitions, healings, soul-awakenings, slowly transforming the inner life of the seeker.

Figure 10 portrays the Master—the soul who, having experienced much meditation and prayer, has aroused kundalini to its full and sustained awakening. In such a soul, the kundalini remains active in sushumna, resembling an upraised serpent—a cobra standing on its tail with its head in the brain stimulating the pituitary-pineal glands, resulting in the permanently opened third eye of the mystic-master.

When Jesus said, "Be ye wise as serpents, but gentle as the dove," it is doubtful he was referring to the crawling creature of Earth, which is no more wise than any of the animals. Such a serpent possesses animal instinct, as do all animals, but no particular wisdom. Jesus must have been referring to the serpent of the Mystery Schools, the initiate who, having awakened kundalini and gained permanent illumination, wore the sign of the upraised cobra on his or

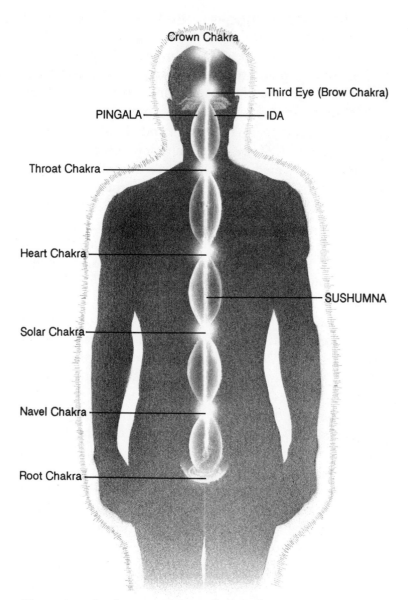

Figure 11. Sushumna, ida and pingala.

her headdress, for the cobra was symbolic of the awakened kundalini.

In the Mystery Schools of antiquity, particularly in Egypt, only the priest-hierophant and Ptah of supreme initiations wore the symbol of the upraised cobra in the headdress (above the third eye) to signify mastery over the god-power of kundalini. Such Master-Initiates were called the _Nagas_. Naga means _the serpent_, the wise one— meaning the one with permanently upraised kundalini. "Be ye wise as the serpent, but gentle as the dove," was an admonition to become wise as the ascended Master, but simultaneously to manifest the gentleness and humility of the dove, symbol of the Holy Spirit.

To complete the mystery of mastery, we must refer to the three vital nerves extending between the root chakra at the base of the spine, and the crown chakra in the head. These three channels (shown in figure 11) are called:

1) _ida_ (_ee_-dah)—the feminine negative channel; the nerve which transports the negative electric nerve force;

2) _pingala_ (_ping_-ga-lah)—the masculine positive nerve channel, carrier of the positive magnetic force;

3) _sushumna_ (shoo-_shoom_-nah)—the etheric nerve running through the spinal cord, the channel conveying the equalized positive and negative forces of ida and pingala.[1]

Both ida and pingala begin at the root of each nostril and spiral down the left and right sides of the spinal column to end in kanda, the etheric "cup" that houses

---

[1]Negative energy means feminine energy while positive refers to masculine energy. Don't confuse the terms with good and bad, but think of them as the positive and negative poles of electricity.

kundalini at the base of the spine. They cross each other at various intervals down the spine, and where they meet and cross there is formed a force center we have called a *chakra*. It is through sushumna in the spinal cord that kundalini will rise, but it usually does not rise until the positive and negative forces of ida and pingala are equalized or balanced. And that is what meditation and prayer are all about, and the breathing techniques we mystics often undertake. We are striving to equalize ida and pingala, therefore opening the way for kundalini to rise naturally up sushumna.

Sushumna, an etheric nerve thread—called by mystics the soul thread—rises out of the root chakra and runs straight up the spinal cord, piercing the base of the skull, the cerebellum, the cerebrum, and the crown chakra. In the crown chakra it becomes the sutratma, or silver cord, and proceeds upward to reach the Oversoul forcefield above your head.

Ida and pingala cross sushumna in the root chakra, the navel chakra, the solar plexus chakra, the heart, throat and brow chakras, and terminate at the gateway to each nostril, but their essence merges in the crown chakra in the head.

During meditation the seeker may be able to raise kundalini completely through sushumna to reach the head centers, or only as far as the solar plexus. Many mystics and initiates are able to raise kundalini partway up the spine during prayers or meditation, but very few attain the mental power for its ultimate ascension—to pierce the medulla oblongata at the base of the skull and enter the brain, stimulating the pituitary-pineal glands and opening the third eye. The chakras normally lie in a state of semi-dormancy, the energy rays folded together or turning downward. But as kundalini rises through sushumna, the rays of force turn upward.

When "manna" from heaven — the spiritual force from the Oversoul — pours down into the physical form, it often passes outward again, leaving no evidence upon the body, bringing no healing or awakening, because the ordinary person, unaware of the chakras and that energy follows thought, makes no effort to arouse these force centers. Therefore they lie in a state of semi-dormancy.

But when you meditate or pray — and become aware of kundalini and the chakras — the mental concentration will often stimulate and awaken kundalini, causing the chakras to become more active. As the rays of the chakric centers turn upward, forming receptive cups, they absorb the downflowing light from the Oversoul, bringing the nectar of the gods to the physical form. "My cup runneth over," sings the Psalmist, referring to the entire auric force-field, which, when filled with grace from on high, radiates spiritual essences.

As mercury rises in a thermometer under the pressure of atmospheric heat, so does the liquid fire of kundalini rise through sushumna under the pressure of psychic heat, which is often activated during prayer or meditation. It travels sometimes slowly, sometimes swift as lightning. When kundalini reaches the medulla oblongata, it is often blocked from entering the third ventricle of the brain because the pineal gland lies dormant over the portal. Unless the pineal is standing erect, kundalini cannot enter the sacred laboratory of the third eye. Denied entrance, it subsides into its home in kanda. When kundalini is aroused to its full intensity, the liquid fire of pingala and the cool water of ida become vapor in sushumna, the soul thread in the spinal cord. The transmuted vapor becomes a mystic dew and, as such, passes into the fourth ventricle of the brain, causing pineal, the male gland, to stand erect.

The erection of the pineal allows the vapor of kundalini to flow into the third ventricle. The aroused masculine pineal begins to project its "love potion" toward the feminine pituitary, wooing its mate. Responding, pituitary releases her own love hormone. The substances meet in the marriage bed of the third ventricle, resulting in the opening of the third eye. The opened third eye raises the seeker into states of altered consciousness, vivid visions, intuitive perceptions. When such an aroused feminine kundalini (the Holy Spirit) is met by a downpouring grace of the masculine Oversoul ("our Father which art in heaven"), the soul has attained illumination, cosmic consciousness. In the ancient Mystery Schools, this marriage of kundalini and the Oversoul was called the *immaculate conception*.

This soul is "saved by grace." Past karma is obliterated by the baptism of Holy Spirit. Mental love has been imbued with divine love. Such a baptism, such an awakening of kundalini, often requires many months, even years. Usually, at the end of a meditation, a small portion of kundalini, having arrived at the crown chakra and having temporarily stimulated the third eye, slowly descends again to kanda, leaving each chakra a portion of its power. Each time a seeker meditates or prays, it raises kundalini closer to the brain. Each chakra is enhanced.

At our present level, the heart and throat chakras are the two most affected, the kundalini often descending only as far down as these two as it departs the third eye area. This explains the emergence of homosexuals so suddenly in our midst in increasing numbers, taking their places often as near-geniuses among us. Though there are undesirables among them just as there are among heterosexuals, the majority exhibit remarkable talents, compassion, and creativity. These are the first faint evidences of a new paradigm evolving in the human race — a clear indication we are headed toward becoming androgynous.

Each moment spent in prayer brings some charge, some dynamic power, up the spine to stimulate the chakras. And each time kundalini is raised, even in part, chakras are affected. They never totally return to their previous state. Each period of meditation brings about some measure of enhancement — for both the chakras and for kundalini. The consciousness, concentrating upon a holy one, such as Lord Jesus or the divine Mary, through a rosary or a meditative chant, balances the positive-negative forces of pingala and ida. The etheric channel of sushumna is gradually cleared of embedded thoughtforms from the past. The protective etheric webs superimposing the chakras are temporarily dissolved. The head centers of the third eye are vitalized, and kundalini, overcoming the downward pull of gravity, is drawn upward through magnetic attraction.

As the disciple becomes the initiate, there comes that magical moment when kundalini remains "upraised," keeping the third eye permanently opened. The baptism of Holy Spirit and grace from our Father will have anointed the soul, and the seeker will have become "the true and perfect serpent," the honed philosopher's stone.

You are so much more than meets the eye. What you see surrounding your dense physical form, the "whole person" (figure 12 on page 40), is representative of the force-fields about you. The monad exists above your head as a tremendous concentration of energy, an energy so tenuous, so ineffable, so radiant, we can only speak of it as divine spirit. The reservoir of divine mind dwelling there is

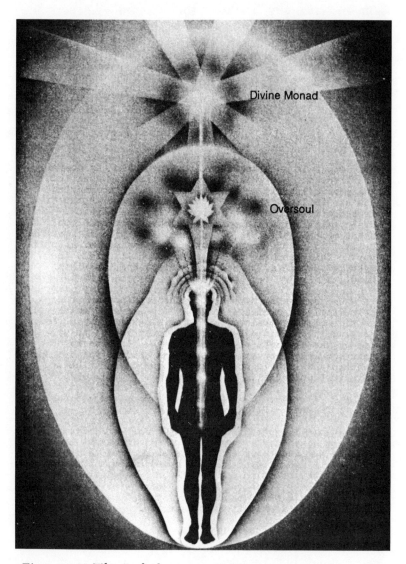

Figure 12. The "whole person." You are more than what meets the eye!

so far above our present understanding as to be incomprehensible to us. We can only depict the monad as a seven-pointed star of light.

The twelve-petaled lotus, which represents the unfolding soul in the causal body, is again a center of concentrated energy. We call it soul energy. This is the "cloud of unknowing," which has been projected from the monad. Over many eons of time, a part of it has evolved into the Oversoul. A lower part has become the soul, some of which has been projected into the world of matter to become the _personality_.

At the end of each incarnation the personality deposits into the forcefield of the Oversoul that part of its Earth experience which has been beautiful and good—so that the soul constantly increases its potential for divinity and omniscience—while the negative or evil essence becomes inherent as characteristics in the seed atoms.

We have given in figure 12 a view of the physical, etheric, astral, mental, causal, and the entire auric force-field, with the sutratma, sushumna, ida, pingala and the chakras. This glimpse may help to plant seeds of knowledge concerning the whole person—divine and human. We have depicted your small self and your greater self—the better to help you understand what happens during the process called death.

If you want to understand the art of dying, it is essentially that you have some knowledge of the various "bodies," and a thorough knowledge of the three permanent seed atoms. Their functioning during the death process is of vital importance. It is also imperative that you are familiar with the chakras, the kundalini, the sushumna, and the sutratma—the silver cord. Without a knowledge of these aspects of your total being, it is not possible to understand the part karma plays in your destiny — whether or not you may be "saved," whether or not you will be called into incarnation again, or whether you will be liberated and "go no more out from the Father's house." Only with such knowledge can a thorough understanding of death, its potential initiation, and your birth into the higher planes be fully comprehended.

Chapter Three.

DEATH, THE TIMELESS MOMENT

ONLY AFTER UNDERSTANDING some of the mysteries can the mystery of death be understood. Now that a synopsis of these profound orthologies has been established, we can at last turn our attention to unravelling the mystery of death.

There is not one of us to whom death is a stranger. We have met death either as the grim reaper or as an angel of light, depending upon our philosophy of life. There are four reasons why knowledge concerning death is among the most vital of all mystical teachings:

1) Every soul, prepared or not, faces the transition called death.

2) Every soul, aware or unaware, witnesses the dawning of the Clear Light of the Void just prior to the moment of leaving the physical body at death. It is at this august moment that the dying pilgrim enters the first phase of the Bardo experience. This is the ultimate moment of the soul's entire incarnation — the foremost and final opportu-

nity. The Clear Light is the gateway to salvation, and initiation, and liberation — the opportunity for "deathbed salvation."

3) This vital opportunity for "salvation from one's sins" — or liberation from one's karma — can be easily missed due to ignorance of its approach, or because of an innate fear of death and the unknown, which could superimpose the supreme light.

4) It is an irretrievable loss, since this incomparable opportunity for liberation (salvation) may not come round again until (after your death) you have traversed the soul journey through the spiritual worlds, have incarnated again, and again face the physical death of your next form — because it is only at the incomparable moment of death that the veil is automatically lifted and the Clear Light offers its saving grace.

Although other opportunities may dawn at various steps along the great wheel of the soul's journey, and although illumination may be attained at any time during meditation or prayer in this present life before you experience death, nature itself offers the greatest opportunity at the ending of each physical incarnation. Failure to recognize the Clear Light because of preconceived religious notions, or because of an innate fear, costs many souls the opportunity to gain spiritual heights at this supreme moment.

There is a science to death — there is a right way to die. There is an art to it. Mastering the techniques of dying makes death a certain opportunity for the ultimate initiation.

Before your last physical birth, while you still resided in the realms of spirit, you or your guardian angel decided it was time to make another journey to Earth and, at the time, you knew the highlights of your mission. (See figure 13 on page 46.) You also knew how long you would remain. The timing of your birth and death were recorded as a built-in cosmic clock in the heart seed atom.

The heart seed atom is part of your cosmic nervous system, so the time for your arrival and departure in each incarnation is set to infinity vibrations. At birth the soul merges with the body through an electromagnetic attraction with a "time release." When the electromagnetic attraction is reversed, the soul automatically gravitates toward higher spheres, seeking release from the prison of the physical form. This soul release is what we call "death." The timing of the cosmic clock can sometimes be changed according to our willpower. We frequently hear of incidents when someone's time may have been extended— someone who apparently faced death, and who experienced a miraculous return to life. Perhaps vital prayers convinced the departing soul (or the guardian angel in charge of his or her departure) that vital work could still be accomplished by the soul if life could be extended.

Suicides disrupt this cosmic timing and reap karmic retribution. They are held, through karmic affinity, to the Earth plane near those from whom they have departed and to whom they owe a debt of karmic service. Suicides are held near the Earth plane and near those they deserted for the full length of time they would have been incarnated in the body. When that time arrives—the time of natural death—a cosmic "time clock" releases the soul from its self-created limitations, and it is allowed to progress into the higher realms, according to its karmic destiny. During

Figure 13. Before you came into your present incarnation, your guardian angel indicated the principal mission awaiting you in your new life.

the years the soul is held near those still on Earth, it must perform every possible service to aid those on Earth through their journey.

Death by suicide assures that the soul, in the majority of cases, _must_ reincarnate to fulfill karmic obligations it attempted to escape, whereas one who fulfills each complete physical incarnation is given a greater opportunity for liberation from the wheel of rebirth. The suicide would miss the opportunity to be "saved" by the Clear Light, for missing the Clear Light is the suicide's greatest punishment—his or her greatest loss. The soul must incarnate again to seek that opportunity. Every soul must seek reincarnation until it experiences immersion in the Clear Light—either at the moment of death or during some incomparable moment, usually during meditation or prayer, either in the body or out of the body.

It would be well to establish a clear meaning of what is meant by _liberation_. The orthodox call it salvation, or being saved from one's sins. We mystics and initiates refer to it as overcoming karma, or liberation from karma. Such a liberation means that, at the moment of death, we are able to merge with the Clear Light of the Void, through which we experience release from our karmic "sins," thus escaping the wheel of birth and death which repeatedly brings us into incarnations in the world of matter.

Such a liberation means that you have overcome the Earth—the desires of the realm of matter. Repentance has evoked such a white light as to cause the dissolution of karmic ties, erase the karmic picture images in the heart seed atom, and, through such an inner baptism, to be purified of past transgressions. Such a powerful repentance, happening at death, is called deathbed salvation.

Figure 14. The emergence of the soul at the time of death is as natural as a soul being born from the womb.

The shedding of the physical form is as natural as a chick emerging from its shell. (See figure 14.) The heart seed atom contains important milestones of the entire incarnation. Thus, at the appointed time, this atom will begin releasing atomic particles or picture images of your approaching death into the bloodstream. The picture images reach the glands. The glands, receiving the death message, begin manufacturing a mysterious substance we call a _death hormone_. The blood carries this hormone throughout the entire form.

The hormone loosens the electromagnetic hold of the physical atoms upon the atoms of the higher bodies. The electromagnetic attraction is gradually reversed, releasing the soul. When this inner release begins, the body reacts to its decreasing supply of life force. Atom after atom slips away in an imperceptible withdrawal from the physical body like slow-falling sand in an hourglass. The deterioration of the physical form also indicates the vitalizing of the inner spiritual form. When the spiritual hourglass has run its course, the soul's time has come. The cosmic key turns in your clock of destiny, and the soul turns toward the spheres from whence it came. The physical body often experiences some kind of illness which becomes terminal.

When death seems obvious, if it is possible you should be returned home where you can be surrounded by familiar scenes, by those who love you, by warmth, compassion and tenderness. Your last Earth memory should be of the faces you love.

In a hospital, even a drugged patient is conscious some of the time. In those moments of lucidity, the dying person may become extremely resentful or feel deserted. Many doctors feel they must give their attention to the living. The nurses, knowing a condition is terminal, fulfill their obligation by making certain the patient receives injections for pain, thus ensuring that the patient will die in a state of unconsciousness. Loved ones visit at the appropriate visiting hours, but shrink from mentioning the approaching death.

People who are left to die in a hospital often have no one to talk to, no one with whom to share fears or anxieties. There are those in-between hours when, lying alone, they experience the desperate need to share with someone who understands. It is not dying itself that they dread. It is the long, lonesome loneliness of it. Every possible effort should be made to have the dying brought home—home, where the faces that smile are filled with genuine affection; where loved ones can sit by the bedside during the final days and hours, and discuss—even with anticipation—the coming life Overthere.

But whether at home or in a hospital, as death nears, drugs that cause unconsciousness should be withheld. Doctors almost always give drugs to the dying, feeling it is their duty. Realizing the patient is terminal, doctors assume death to be painful, and feel obliged to see the patient pass in peace, which to the medical profession means a state of unconsciousness.

But as death approaches, the death process itself often blocks the sensation of pain. The death hormone, entering the sympathetic nervous system, usually frees the body from pain. Fluids in the cerebrospinal nervous system automatically accelerate, releasing kundalini and unfolding extrasensory awareness.

Thus death is usually approached without physical pain and, unless suffering is obvious and relief is absolutely necessary, drugs which cause unconsciousness should be withheld as the moment of death approaches so that the pilgrim may experience death in full consciousness. You can explain to the doctor that the departing has requested to die at home, and if possible, to pass in a conscious state.

If consciousness-blocking drugs are given, they may so alter consciousness that the soul misses the highlights of this most important moment, this supreme adventure. Drugs may block the consciousness from viewing the Clear Light of the Void and cause the individual to miss the vital opportunity for soul salvation. The pilgrim may also miss the opportunity for arousing from the death coma to speak to loved ones, and will not be able to describe the spirit forms of loved ones who have come, or the heavenly visions and scenes unfolding before his or her eyes.

Physicians are aware of two drugs which can be given which reputedly block pain but still allow the pilgrim to experience death in full consciousness. One is called the _Brompton cocktail_. The other is _Zeneperin_. Both were suggested to me by medical doctors. Do discuss these with your family physician.

To digress a moment, you may also want to have in your files a copy of a _Living Will_. This is a legal form, signed by yourself and two witnesses, which requests that, in the event you become terminal, your doctor is requested not to keep you forcibly "alive" by machinery. He or she is to allow you to die with dignity, and avoid a struggle of keeping the physical form functioning through mechanical means. A copy should be in your file at the offices of your doctor and your attorney, and in your own personal files. A legal form of this Living Will may be obtained by sending a request and a donation to:

EUTHANASIA EDUCATIONAL COUNCIL
CONCERN FOR DYING
250 West 57th Street
New York, NY 10107

There are certain steps to be taken to help the dying attain the potential initiation. Mantrams may be chanted during the hours that precede death. Those assisting the transition may chant the familiar OM-MANI-PADME-HUM mantram, or the one sacred word OM. Or they may repeat some form of the rosary, a Christian chant. The chant should be spoken in a soft undertone, otherwise the sound could be annoying and disturbing rather than soothing.

The dying should be placed facing the east when practical or possible. If incense is desired, only sandalwood should be burned. Catholics will call a priest to perform the holy unction and hear confession. Others will engage in prayer. Masons may perform a certain ritual to guide the soul toward a sure and higher resurrection.

A taped Bardo ritual may be played. Mystics who belong to Mystery Schools such as Astara or the Rosicrucians will often read a specially prepared Bardo ritual or play a Bardo ritual tape to guide the departing soul through the veil, helping the pilgrim avoid an encounter with the dwellers on the threshold — the thoughtforms of the pilgrim's own mind, created through the years of the life just ended. This ritual should be read or played at the bedside of the dying, whether at home or in a hospital.[1]

---

[1] Write to Astara, Box 5003, Upland, CA. 91786 for information concerning such a tape.

The words are carefully planned to soothe away fear, to help guide the consciousness into full awareness of the approaching Clear Light; to bring to remembrance the importance of concentrating upon this Light; or to help attain liberation — or salvation — at the time of passing.

It is important that there be absolute silence in the death room except for the words of the Bardo ritual. Those who cannot contain their grief should depart the death chamber so that the dying pilgrim not be distracted. The pilgrim should be given full opportunity to focus total consciousness upon the approaching Clear Light, the ultimate moment of spiritual attainment.

Loud lamenting may cause distress, distracting the pilgrim at the supreme moment when complete awareness should be centered upon what is occurring during the transitional spiritual birth. The dying is the one to be considered. Even though he or she appears to be lying in a coma, unconscious of the surroundings, it is not true. The pilgrim will be entering an expanded state of consciousness and _can_ hear the words of a Bardo death ritual. Also heard will be the family arguments as to who will inherit dad's gold watch, the family silverware, mother's jewelry, whether or not the estate has been fairly divided, or whether the preferred funeral home was selected. Such discussions have no place in a death room — only silence or a Bardo ritual.

The Science of Death

Let us say that your body has grown elderly and weary with the long passage of Earth time. You have entered a terminal illness. You realize full well that you lie upon your deathbed. The heart seed atom has begun to release the death message into the bloodstream to the glands, which begin releasing the death hormone. Soul electricity begins to escape, loosening the threads of the silver cord, the spiritual umbilical cord. The soul, answering the magnetic attraction of the higher spheres, begins a movement toward the brain.

Now the death process does not differ a great deal from the birth process. You know that during the hours of childbirth, the birth canal gradually opens, allowing the downward passage of the infant form. The walls of the womb and vagina begin to expand to allow passage of the little form outward.

In a similar fashion, your physical form becomes the womb from which the spirit-soul must escape at the time of death, at the time of the soul's return to the higher sphere—for death is truly a second birth. The sutratma-sushumna becomes the birth canal through which the soul must depart. The crown chakra at the top of the head begins to expand just as does the physical womb-vagina, the better to allow release of the spirit.

Life force gravitates like slow-moving lightning toward the brain. The life force first leaves the feet and legs. They turn cold, and all color departs. Then the hands and arms are affected, and the nails turn purple, reflecting the change in the blood. The breathing may become labored and the eyes dimmed. These signs may be observed by those watching—signs indicating death is near. But the watchers will be unable to observe that the pineal gland is becoming extremely active, that the brain in the skull is becoming porous as the crown chakra opens and expands. The soul is passing upward through the birth

canal of the sutratma—the silver cord. It is escaping from
the womb of the physical body. Kundalini is awakening
and preparing for its upward journey. And the three permanent seed atoms are preparing for their departure.

As kundalini moves upward, the usual procedure is
for the emotional seed atom in the solar plexus to depart
first, as the life force reaches the solar plexus. (See figure
15 on page 56.) When the atom exits via the silver cord,
that is when all pain ceases. Since the mental and heart
seed atoms still are intact in the physical form, the pilgrim
may lie in a death coma indefinitely—sometimes days,
sometimes weeks, but usually only a few moments.

With the upward passage of the life force and the
kundalini, rather than sinking into oblivion, you become
increasingly psychic. You become aware that you are not
dying at all; rather your consciousness is becoming increasingly "alive," and awareness is expanding.

At the moment kundalini arrives at the crown chakra
and strikes the pituitary-pineal center in the brain, the
third eye opens, just as when you experience the ultimate
in meditation. It is at this moment, just prior to death,
that you experience the first phase of the _Bardo_. This—the
ultimate moment of the entire incarnation—is the
moment when there dawns the Clear Light of the Void,
the gateway to salvation and initiation. The life force is
condensed in the third eye; the pituitary-pineal glands
have accelerated to their full intensity. (See figure 16 on
page 58.) This is the supreme moment when one or all of
several experiences may occur:

1) You may arouse from apparent unconsciousness to bid
farewell to the loved ones around you;

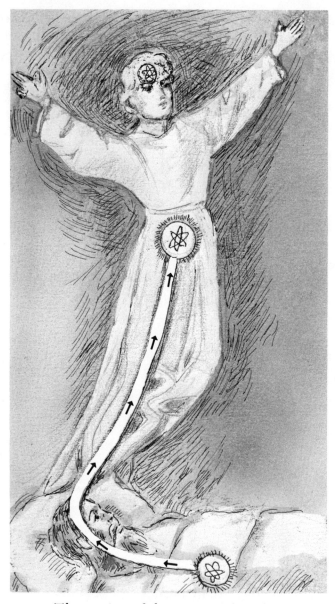

Figure 15. The passing of the emotional seed atom.

2) You may see the spirits of long dead loved ones waiting to welcome you, or deities whom you have worshipped assisting your release;

3) You may see splendid landscapes and hear beautiful music;

4) You may be engulfed in an all-encompassing bliss, and spiritual ecstasy may pervade your consciousness.

After describing the spirits waiting to welcome you — or even some deity, such as Lord Jesus or the Virgin Mary — or describing the heavenly scenes or music, or attempting to describe the all-encompassing bliss of the Clear Light, you will probably pass into the death coma. This indicates the glandular chemicals have centered around the pineal gland, striving to free the mental seed atom. Freed, the atom departs via the crown chakra, passing upward through the silver cord to anchor in the brain area of the newly forming spiritual body. Your physical form is experiencing clinical death, but your consciousness is becoming more alive. The clinical death process lasts from six minutes to half an hour.

A doctor, seeking to determine whether death has occurred, would be unable to discover a heartbeat, or a pulse, and would pronounce you dead. But the sutratma remains intact, and the heart seed atom has not yet escaped. It may follow shortly after the consciousness ceases, after the mental atom departs.

With the passing of the mental and the emotional seed atoms, you are no longer conscious on the Earth plane nor can your physical form experience any sensation or feeling. A psychic would see emanations of a white cloud, or shining smoke, escaping from the head area of the

Figure 16. The release of the mental seed atom.

dying pilgrim. Waves of color, like a miniature aurora borealis, ripple upward, flashing with indescribable hues. The entire spiritual form is gradually taking shape, held to the dead physical form by a vital electric cord (the sutratma) which extends from the brain of the dying pilgrim to a point between the shoulders of the newly forming spiritual body.

Light around the physical head gradually diminishes as the clouds of smoky emanations undulate and expand — until the features of a face begin to appear in the spirit form. The face will resemble that of the dying pilgrim. It will be the same face, but the lines of care and tension are gone. It may appear younger and more serene.

It is at this point when there dawns the _Secondary Light_. This light is dazzling but not so blinding as the first Clear Light of the Void. This is a second opportunity for salvation and initiation. Each soul reacts according to its own understanding of God, death and immortality. (I shall describe the Secondary Light in full later.) _The Secondary Light will dawn a half hour after clinical death, or a half hour after a doctor pronounces you dead_. The heart seed atom may have made its escape, or it may require a delay in the body because the astral form builds more slowly for some than for others. This is when the organs of the physical body actually begin to die. This period lasts from one to fifteen hours. The silver cord is gradually loosening. One by one the threads are breaking. The emotional and the mental seed atoms in the newly forming astral body are extremely active. It is their influence which is building the structure of your new astral form. Your astral body will be built according to the picture images now flowing into the pattern body of your new astral body.

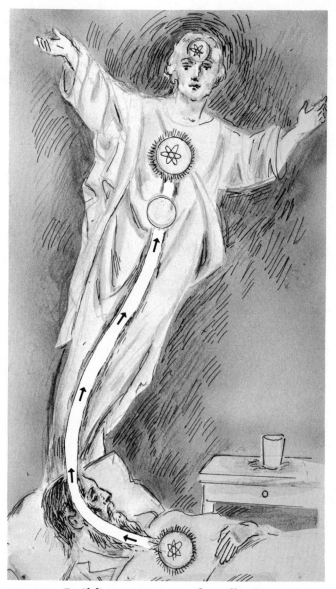

Figure 17. Building a transcendentally beautiful astral form.

I previously mentioned that the etheric pattern forms first in the matrix of the mother's womb when pregnancy occurs on the physical plane. Just so, there is now formed an archetypical etheric pattern above your head, responding to the outflowing influence of the mental seed atom and the emotional seed atom. This is the _kama rupa_, or the _lower astral body_. It is built according to your lowest emotional manifestations during life. The desires that dominated your physical existence will now act as the causative agent in forming the pattern upon which the atoms of your newly forming astral body will adhere.

Thus your new form will be built according to your lowest desires. If you possessed undesirable habits, such as smoking, drinking, or drugs, the atoms of your new spiritual form will be imbued with the essence of these vibrations. Although these may not be _evil_ habits, they often block the potential of high spiritual atoms. If you thought bestial thoughts, or were consumed with hatred, greed, selfishness, negativity, or evil, your astral form will now respond to the influence of those thoughts as the picture images pour out of your emotional and mental seed atoms into the substance of your new lower desire body.

If you expressed few carnal desires, watched your thoughts carefully, and expressed only that which was pure and beautiful, the mental and emotional seed atoms now respond by building a transcendentally beautiful astral form. (See figure 17.) It is during this time that the organs of the physical body are dying, requiring from one to fifteen hours, as stated.

Only after the newly born spiritual form is fully built will the heart seed atom make its escape. The atoms of the physical form, building in the matrix of the mother's womb on the physical plane, require nine months to be

Figure 18. With the departure of the heart seed atom, the silver cord breaks, releasing the spiritual form completely to its new life.

completed. But a newly arisen spiritual form requires from one to fifteen hours to be completed. These could be called the hours of spiritual labor, the birth pangs of spiritual birth.

When the new spiritual form is completed—either beautiful or marred, responding to the pattern of your thoughts and emotions—only then will the heart seed atom depart. It may depart immediately with the cessation of the heartbeat, or linger several hours, as the astral form gains its new birth, just as some physical births are rapid while others require many hours of labor. Its departure signals the actual moment or time of death, though a doctor may have pronounced death hours earlier. With the departure of the heart seed atom, the silver cord breaks, releasing the spiritual form completely, as shown in figure 18. The Secondary Light does not dawn until about half an hour after the heart seed atom departs and the silver cord breaks, signaling final death.

In no case should embalming, burial or cremation occur before a period of three days following death. The sutratmic silver cord may still be attached to the form, held by the heart seed atom, which is often slow to depart. Also, the soul is experiencing the Bardo journey of the afterdeath state. The body should be held for three days in a refrigerated room, in total peace and quiet. Only afterward should activity occur, such as preparation for burial.

Numerous Types of Death

It should be obvious that only one type of death has been described—that of an elderly person, dying a natural death or from a terminal illness. There are other types, such as sudden death from heart attack, murder or accident. But in all cases, even death by violent accident, the procedure is the same. The heart seed atom is the last to depart, taking the "movie" of your entire incarnation with it. The heart atom may depart suddenly—as is usually the case in the death of an initiate—or it may linger for a full three days, as in the death of an average person.

The initiate or dedicated mystic usually departs the dying form "in the twinkling of an eye," as St. Paul describes, taking all three seed atoms instantaneously. But the usual spirit birth requires three days, during which time the body should be placed in a quiet atmosphere so that the soul, experiencing the journey of the Bardo, may experience every opportunity to face the dwellers on the threshold, recognize them as thoughtforms, and proceed toward the highest achievable plane of light on celestial spheres. I'll discuss these things in more depth in the next chapter.

Chapter Four

THE BARDO
AND THE JOURNEY OF THE SOUL

WHAT IS THE _Bardo_? It is the afterdeath journey of the soul on its way to its home in the higher spheres. Before the soul actually awakens Overthere, the pilgrim faces a mental journey. Call it a judgment if you will. The soul will find its abode—whether on a high plane or a low—depending on how it reacts to the initiation tests of the Bardo judgment journey. And its reaction usually reflects the pattern of the life just ended.

The Bardo has three phases. The first is the dawning of the Clear Light of the Void. The second is the viewing of the Secondary Light. The third is the lonesome valley of the judgment.

Initiates (the seekers of light) will see before them, just prior to the moment of death, the dazzling, blinding Clear Light of the Void, shown in figure 19 on page 66. Since their own inner light will harmonize with the high voltage of the Clear Light, these souls will merge with it.

Figure 19. The Clear Light of the Void.

They will be "saved." They will be liberated. They will be freed from remaining karma or "sins." They will be released from "the wheel of life and death," never required to incarnate again in a mortal physical form. They will have become immortal—or not subject to mortality. These initiates will escape the Bardo judgment altogether, being taken immediately after death into the high planes of celestial paradise. For these evolved souls, there will be no sleeping, no loss of consciousness.

Others—souls who have led good lives but have not been actively involved in light seeking—unable to merge with the high voltage of the Clear Light, will merge with the Secondary Light. They will waken surrounded by loved ones. They, too, will not experience the third phase—the Bardo judgment. The opening eyes will view the spiritual surroundings with incredible wonder and awe. They may or may not be required to incarnate again. They will awaken on one of the astral planes, with innumerable opportunities to progress to higher planes.

Still others—people who were filled with every carnal thought and desire—will enter immediately the third stage of the Bardo or what we call the lonesome valley of the judgment. This third Bardo may be experienced while the pilgrim still hovers in the death chamber, resting in a dream consciousness. Or, before entering the Bardo journey in consciousness, the newly born soul, still sleeping, may be borne away to a haven of rest by an angel of mercy. But whether in the death room or in a spiritual retreat, the consciousness of these souls passes into a hypnotic swoon through which they enter the third phase of the Bardo.

One recognized phase of the Bardo is the shadow-show of reliving the episodes of the past life and perhaps even some scenes of previous lives. This record is the Book

Figure 20. During the Bardo, the scenes of the past life flash before the memory.

of Life "movie" which unreels from its projection room in the heart seed atom. The soul life passes in review. (See figure 20.) As it flashes before consciousness, the pilgrim will begin to understand why certain things happened during the mortal life just ended — and why some did not. We hear much now about regression therapy, and how such an experience often awakens the consciousness to an awareness of many previously unexplained fears, loves, hopes. Such is this afterdeath phase of the Bardo — a soul journey into self-understanding.

We initiates and mystics strive constantly during our meditations and prayers to raise kundalini and experience the ultimate illumination. But just prior to the death of our physical form, kundalini rises naturally. The natural release of this awakening creative force results in the three phases of the Bardo. The effect is not unlike the "trip" produced by the drug LSD (or other hallucinatory drugs) upon the physical brain and brain cells. Candidates of the Mysteries also experienced this effect during initiation into the Mystery Schools of antiquity.

The First Phase: The Clear Light

Let's consider now in greater detail the three phases of this Bardo journey. The first phase of the Bardo — the first moments of kundalini rising — heralds the dawning of the Clear Light of ultimate liberation. As the empirical consciousness of the objective world fades and kundalini rises through sushumna, the initiate may pass into what would be recognized as a kind of hypnotic trance; not a descent into unconsciousness but an ascent into superconsciousness. The subjective mind opens to the dawning of the Clear Light of the Void.

Now what is this Clear Light and what is this Void? The Clear Light is the reflection of consciousness devoid of all darkness, all limitations. It is that which is beyond all human description since it possesses neither height, width, depth nor weight. It is purified perfection shining like a dazzling sun upon the mirror of your mind, as your consciousness passes from the limitations of brain bondage to expanded awareness. Your mind must be freed of all darkness and all limitation if the purified perfection of the Clear Light is to shine clearly upon the mirror of it.

If there is darkness within the consciousness, it is reflected on the mirror of your mind and the mirror cannot then reflect the radiance of the Clear Light itself. At this moment when the Clear Light dawns, the mind is like a mirror and *only* when it is cleared of karmic obstructions can the mind reflect the ultimate light of reality. This is why it is so difficult for most of us to imagine that we may merge with the Clear Light, because the mind must be completely cleared of all karmic darkness.

What is the Void? It is truly not a void as we imagine a void to be. To us, a void is a center of nothingness. But the Clear Light of the Void is the absolute *All*. We call it the Void because it is beyond description. The Void summarizes its beingness since it has no width, depth, height, center, color, weight, form or name. We could call it God since both are indescribable. And actually one would not be too far amiss to speak of the Clear Light of the Void as coming face to face with God—in the form of the light of lights.

In the Void, the initiate's consciousness—freed of all darkness and limitations—experiences oneness with that which is beyond all consciousness. In such a state, there is momentarily no time, space, emotion or action. There is only being-in-bliss.

Those who are able to remain in united at-one-ment with this light experience deathbed salvation. At this moment, they gain liberation from their karma. They have broken the cyclic rhythm of the wheel of birth and death and need go no more out from the Father's house. "Him that overcometh will I make a pillar in the temple of my God, and he shall go no more out: and I will write upon him the name of my God, and the name of the city of my God . . . which cometh down out of heaven from my God; and I will write upon him my new name" (Revelation 3:12). The duration of this exalted state varies according to the spiritual status of the individual, lasting anywhere from a minute to several hours to several days. Usually the initiate is transformed in the twinkling of an eye—instantly.

Many mystics and light seekers will experience the Clear Light ecstasy at the moment of death. (See figure 21 on page 72.) They will experience instant liberation. They will merge with the Clear Light, escaping all phases of the Bardo. They are liberated from the pathway of normal evolution, freed from karma. They need come back no more into a form of matter unless they wish to do so. Many times the Great Ones are sent back to help humanity in its struggle in upward evolution, but such a teacher comes not of necessity. They come because they wish to be of service.

To see this Clear Light of the Void at the moment of death, you need to prepare for it during life. There are

Figure 21. The Clear Light ectasy.

rules you must follow to accomplish this seeing, this tuning in, this merging with the Clear Light:

1) You must cultivate a serene, quiet mind during meditation. Not that the meditation must be absolutely complete and perfect in every way, but you should quiet your mind as much as possible, attempting to see the Clear Light during your lifetime. Which means that you are either attempting to updraw the kundalini and experience the baptism of Holy Spirit, or downdraw grace from the Oversoul.

2) You should pray daily. And truly feel a deep devotion and reverence toward the deity you are addressing — Jesus, Mary, Buddha, Shiva, God Himself. Such dedication will stir up the gift of God within (kundalini), and will eventually bring the sought-for baptism of Holy Spirit, although you may not be aware of it in your conscious mind.

3) Attempt to destroy all your karmic bonds. This implies that you try to right all your wrongs. This means you should seek forgiveness from those you have hurt, even those now dwelling on the Otherside — and you should express forgiveness to those who have wronged you. Again, supplication may be expressed in prayer form. Realize you have probably created many monstrous thoughtforms, and these should be destroyed by thinking extraordinarily beautiful thoughts, especially prayers, the better to purify the dark thoughts of the past. "Overcome evil with good," said the Master.

4) Attempt to die in full consciousness. It *is* possible to see the Clear Light even if your consciousness is drugged, but you are apt to miss it. If your consciousness is drugged, you

may be totally unaware of the Clear Light when it dawns, and pass out of the body seeing only the Secondary Light, which comes just after passing from the body.

5) Avoid temptations of wrong doing. Recognizing that you are building, during life, the spirit body which you will inhabit, and that the atoms of that body will be built according to your thoughts and emotions as they are recorded in the heart seed atom, you should recognize wrong actions as they approach in this life and avoid them altogether. If you are tempted to do that which you think is wrong, remember that you may meet the mistake during your Bardo journey. So, once you become aware of the coming of the Clear Light and what will happen at the moment of death, you subconsciously tend to avoid thoughts and actions that may have karmic attachments.

However, be very sure not to let society entangle you in a "guilt trap." Much the world labels "wrong" may be very "right" in the sight of God. Always consider your motive for whatever the world may judge as a wrong. If your motive was love, and if no one was hurt in the transaction, then don't let the judgment of society make you feel guilty of a wrong. Clear it with God. If you feel right with God, then never mind what the world thinks. The world is seldom qualified to judge the true record written in the heart—only God can read that Book of Life. Only God will judge, and He first judges motives, not actions.

A word of caution about meditation seems advisable. Many light seekers give up meditation because they see many fearful forms while they are sitting quietly. Frightening faces rise before them—or scenes that are not pleasant.

They see no reason to continue meditation if subjected to such experiences. May I admonish you not to cease. Beginning meditations often have their unpleasant aspect, but it is excellent that you are coming face-to-face with some of your own thoughtforms now, while you are still living, and you are being offered an opportunity to destroy them. If you recognize these faces and forms as thoughtform dwellers on the threshold, seize this opportunity to destroy them now, rather than facing them during the Bardo journey at death. Their presence at that time could be a major reason you may miss the Clear Light initiation—because they seem real, and could cause distraction when you should be concentrating on merging with the Clear Light.

Each time such a form arises during meditation, keep surrounding it in pure white light until you have completely dissipated it. Recognize it as a thoughtform and not an actual reality. Be aware that the spinal column is the filing cabinet of thoughtforms. When you begin to meditate or habitually pray, the kundalini begins to stir. With such stirrings, a portion of its power could enter sushumna in the spinal cord. As it enters from the area of the root chakra, it begins to dislodge thoughtforms filed away there. They rise into the consciousness during meditation. Some take gruesome shapes and appear actually to be alive. But they are no more real than your favorite actor when you watch him play a role in a movie.

Eventually you will meet and destroy all thoughtforms from the past, all the threshold dwellers. Eventually your meditations will be freed of such disturbances. With your victory over the thoughtforms, you begin to see ever and ever clearer reflections of the pure white light.

I think I must have experienced some part of my Bardo journey when I was a child because I saw monstrous visions and figures while lying awake at night. If you have read my book *Remembering*,[1] you will recall that I had a terrifying experience with a cow, after which I began to be unable to fall asleep at night. I would see forming high up in the corner of my room the figure of a cow—or worse, a bull. In the ensuing drama, I was always fleeing, the animal chasing me, drawing ever nearer. I was absolutely terrified as I watched the monster close in on me. In the flight, which was enacted as a scene before my eyes, I was perpetually looking back to gauge how close was the pursuing beast. Just at the moment of encounter and assault, I always suddenly turned to face the monster and stood still to meet the impact. And just as suddenly, the animal also stood still. As I faced it, preparing for battle, its form slowly would begin to disintegrate, as if made of sand. And I would stare at the sand heap in utter amazement, wondering what had happened. Lying there, I was always bewildered that I had been so mysteriously saved.

Of course, my own fears had built a thoughtform of the dreaded monster and I had allowed it to continue frightening me over and over and over. I was living a Bardo drama, a dread, a fear. "The thing which I greatly feared is come upon me. That of which I was afraid is come unto me" (Job 3:25).

And that is exactly what can happen. That which you fear can certainly come upon you in the shape of a thoughtform you yourself have created. It can pursue and

---

[1]Earlyne Chaney, *Remembering—The Autobiography of a Mystic* (Upland, CA: Astara, 1974).

frighten you until you learn that it is nothing more than a devil you have created yourself. Once you realize your own thoughts can create a bevy of devils, then you are liberated from that fear and that thoughtform. That's what liberation in the Bardo is all about—being liberated from our fears, devil thoughtforms, sins, and karma.

The Clear Light comes to _all_ just prior to the moment of death—not as deathbed forgiveness "through the Church," as orthodox priesthood would have us believe, but as an opportunity for deathbed salvation for _all_ God's children, regardless the church of their faith. Buddhist, Moslem, Hindu, Christian, Jew, saint, sinner, poor, rich, good or bad—ALL are offered the Clear Light as a gift of God's saving grace. At the moment of death, you are indeed going to meet your Maker, your father/mother creator. They are coming as a Clear White Light, and in this light you will stand either vindicated or guilty.

Forgiveness

Probably the most important part and point of the entire Bardo journey is forgiveness. To the degree that you have forgiven those who wronged you, to that same degree will there now shine from within you an inner light. And the degree of inner light will determine whether or not your soul can merge permanently with the dazzling purity of the Clear Light, and be saved. Such a saving means you will escape migrating temporarily to a lower plane of soul darkness. It also means you have forever broken the thought pattern of karma that has held you to a wheel of birth and death in the field of matter. You have become immortal. That is the importance of forgiveness.

If you forgave those who sinned against you, the Father—the Clear Light—will now forgive you. If you loved your enemies and did good to those who hated you, your inner light will fuse with God's light. "With what measure you mete, it will be measured unto you" (Matthew 7:2). This is the place and time of your judgment and you will be judged by how thoroughly you have forgiven your adversaries.

If you have wronged someone and have not made right that wrong, if you did not seek for and obtain their forgiveness, you will now face the Clear Light which will judge you accordingly. If it is possible to do so while still living, seek out the ones you have wronged and beg forgiveness.

I am reminded of a friend who had an experience with forgiveness in a Bardo journey. Let us call him Rev. John Smith. Rev. Smith was quite a mystic. He conducted many seminars based on metaphysical Bible interpretations—and published similar writings.

He decided to experiment with LSD. This was during the years when everybody seemed to think it was the "in" thing to do. But Rev. Smith had a bad trip. In the beginning, he experienced the "high." During that exalted state, he saw standing before him, a distance away, the shining figure of the great Master Jesus. Elated, Rev. Smith rushed forward to fall at the feet of the Master. But just before he reached the Master, the figure of his deceased father stepped between, blocking his way. Try as he might, he could not pass beyond his father to reach the Master. Suddenly he recalled that he had grievously wronged his father during life and had never sought his forgiveness.

He awakened from the LSD trip feeling his life was now a shambles. He felt that since his father had passed to the Otherside, he would not be able to obtain his forgiveness until he himself arrived there. We tried to persuade him to seek forgiveness even now. We reminded him that his father could hear him, and he should ask his forgiveness in moments of prayer. Since he truly felt remorseful, his father would assuredly respond. But Rev. Smith refused to even consider it. He held doggedly to the notion that it was "too late." His entire life changed.

Suddenly he reverted from mysticism to orthodox fundamentalism, fanatically ranting about eternal hellfire and damnation. He reproached my husband and me severely for continuing our mystical pathway. He felt that since he had seen "hell" during his LSD trip, he would surely go there unless he saved others, and his new concept of salvation was to preach the fear of God, eternal damnation, and hellfire. His life was shattered. Often he spoke of being doomed to hell because of the wrong he had committed. The guilt changed him from a happy, outgoing teacher of light into a moody, depressed, fear-filled, bombastic preacher.

That is why drugs are often such a dreadful risk. The bad trips can be a complete disaster, harming the soul, the emotions and the personality. Most people who take drugs do not realize they have been on a synthetic Bardo journey. The figure who stepped between Rev. Smith and the Christ was only a thoughtform of his dad—a thoughtform _he himself had created_ because of his own guilty conscience. Forgiveness is the fundamental teaching of initiation in the Clear Light. Forgive—and you shall be forgiven.

In the Sermon on the Mount, Jesus spoke of it. He said, "Therefore, if thou bring thy gift to the altar, and there rememberest that thy brother hath ought against thee, leave there thy gift before the altar and go thy way. First be reconciled to thy brother — and then come and offer thy gift" (Matthew 5:23,24). If you expect your soul to merge with the Clear Light at the moment of death, make sure you have forgiven or have sought forgiveness. If you have not done so, go now and make things right and then come and bring the gift of your lifetime — of your incarnation — to the altar, and it will be accepted by the Clear Light. In this sense, you are going to be judged in this Clear Light exactly as you, yourself, judged others.

There is a biblical story which tells of a Master with many servants. A servant came one day to the Master pleading forgiveness from his debts to the Master, saying he could not pay. Now the Master could have had him thrown into prison until his debts were paid, but he forgave the servant his debts. The grateful servant went his way and met a lesser servant who owed him a debt. But the first servant refused to forgive the debt of the second, and had him thrown into prison. The Master, hearing of this deed, sent for the first servant, reprimanding him harshly. "You wicked servant," he said, "I forgave you your debts. Why could you not have forgiven your debtor? You must now be thrown into prison until you pay your debts to me."

Thus will the Clear Light deal with you. If you refuse to forgive your debtors, so will you not be forgiven at the time of the Clear Light. Seek forgiveness, forgive those who have harmed you and seek forgiveness from those you have harmed. Make it right with your "Lord" or the divine law. "With what measure you mete, it will now be measured unto you" (Matthew 18:32–34).

The Second Phase: Secondary Light

Most light seekers are familiar with the white light and how to make it a practical part of their lives, mentally surrounding themselves daily in an aura of its essence and purity. Therefore, it is possible that many seekers will merge completely with the first dawning of the Clear Light at the moment of death and pass the tests of the highest initiation. If you are unable to unite with its brilliance, you may recognize the Secondary Light and still gain initiation. This light may be more comfortable and not so ineffable.

If you are a pilgrim of Secondary Light, you have not attained complete liberation. While you are lying in a state of hypnotic trance on the Bardo trip—a trip taken totally in consciousness—you will begin to experience unusual sensations in the newly forming astral body. Remember, kundalini will already have risen naturally through sushumna and will have opened your third eye. You may have been so apprehensive about death that you are totally unaware of this happening. Or you may have been unable to merge with the blinding brilliance of the first Clear Light and are now experiencing the Secondary Light, meaning that kundalini is active in your spine.

You will be aware of the actual biological processes occurring in the depths of your being—the heat of the rising kundalini, the electromagnetic power of the chakras as they respond to the newly released psychic force. Remember, the chakras are force centers of the higher bodies, superimposing the endocrine glands of the physical form. It is a perfectly natural process to experience this uprising kundalini at the time of death. Strange sounds and sights also begin to arise. You may be aware of incredibly beautiful music or you may begin to witness visions of magnificent figures, wavering faces and scenes. You may become totally aware of how psychic you are becoming. Now, remember, you are still lying in a state of Bardo trance. This is the time to remember the death teachings you are learning here, it is not a time to glory in your unfolding psychic powers.

Just as any worthy teacher or guru, during life, will admonish the disciple to reach for the summit of cosmic illumination rather than focus on unfolding psychic powers, so do we now emphasize keeping your attention, during death, focused upon the very highest possibility of spiritual illumination. If, during life, you become enamored with your psychic powers, you are apt to bask in your glory rather than continuing to seek the highest form of spiritual illumination—which is intuitive perception or clairsentience. A good teacher constantly warns the seeker to beware of this glamorous entrapment. You must aim for the summit of cosmic illumination and, in so doing, psychic powers will automatically unfold as a by-product of the ultimate goal. Accept them, then, only as such.

The same is true during the Bardo journey. Remember the mystical teachings. Be aware of the unfolding psychic powers but keep reaching for the heights of cosmic consciousness. The surest means of attaining that goal is to focus attention on the one you revered most as your spiritual "savior" or teacher during life—Jesus the Christ, Mary the Blessed Mother, Guatama Buddha, Moses, Siva, Vishnu, Krishna, Zoroaster, Mohammed—the teacher who warranted your highest love and respect.

If you are acquainted with the Bardo process, the figures that begin rising—the faces that flash before you, the forms that you see — these visionary creatures arouse no awe or alarm. You will remember that these figures are thoughtforms, they are the dwellers on the threshold and are no more real than figures upon a television screen. Remember that these figures come from within yourself and they reflect your own thought processes. They will arouse no fear because the figures that rise in the Secondary Light are beautiful, symbolic visions. (See figure 22 on page 84.) Most will be hallucinatory, but they are still completely beautiful in every way.

You will remember that they are created by the karmic reflections of good actions committed by yourself while in the physical form — reflections of your benevolent beautiful thoughts. During the Secondary Light of the Bardo journey, every good thought, every kindness, every prayer becomes some kind of magnificent thoughtform pouring in upon you and merging toward you. If, for instance, you constantly meditated upon some mantram, the power of the repeated sound will now enfold you. The thoughtform you constantly visualized during meditation and prayer will have taken root and grown into full blossom. It is indescribable, the power of these mystical chants and prayers, and that great power will now lift you up and up and up. The forms of the chant will rise before you — even the words of the chant or prayers will keep reappearing. They may take various shapes and sizes but they will pass in a delightful and unbroken panorama.

If you are an enlightened soul, these visions will assume the forms of higher deities, Masters or angels, and, "accepting one as your Savior," you will pass out of the second phase of the Bardo and into the higher planes, escaping the third phase altogether. For instance, if you are a Christian and have meditated upon Jesus the Christ,

Figure 22. The figure and thoughtforms that rise in the Secondary Light are beautiful, symbolic visions.

you will see a thoughtform of Him constantly rising before you, a thoughtform offering to save you. If you attempt to merge with that form, or place your hand in his extended hand, the light of the form itself will carry you out of the hypnotic stage of the Bardo into the spheres of the high astral, or even into the planes of paradise. You will awaken from your hypnotic trance—your Bardo trip—on this plane of glory. You will have accepted Jesus as your Savior in a cosmic sense far beyond that which is understood by the fundamentalists who make so much of the term.

The Third Phase: Valley of the Judgment

If you are not a light seeker, forms of hazy hues will begin to gather around the beautiful figures which reflect the good you have done. The light forms will now begin to fade away, to be overcast by shadows—gradually taking on the aspect of homeliness, ugliness, fearsomeness, darkness—until they fade into various monstrous shapes. Some assume giant proportions, some are more fearful, some are gruesome.

As these slowly begin to form—representing the dark thoughtforms you created—it is as if someone pressed a magic button. A feeling of vacuity engulfs you as if suddenly the power upon which you float dissolves, and all is empty, vacant, devoid of light. The expanded awareness bounds back into its limitations and impinges upon a point within your being. If you refused to turn to the light and lived by your greed, carnality, and so forth, you face the lonesome valley of the judgment.

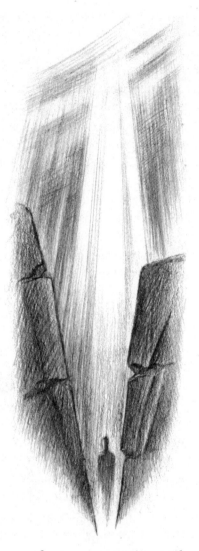

Figure 23. Down, down your awareness plunges, until you stand alone in a secret hall of a dim cavern, deep within your own being. You are experiencing the lonesome Valley of Judgment, the third phase of the Bardo.

Down, down, your awareness plunges. Down, down, into a deep abyss, your mind tumbling over a precipice into a labyrinth, until you stand alone in a secret hall of a dim cavern deep within your own being. (See figure 23.) All joys, sorrows, ambitions, hopes, despairs and aspirations now emerge in the gathering shadows. Slowly even that diminishes until all that is left is your mind, gathered into a point of awareness and focused deep inside yourself, as if poised on the head of a pin. There it balances for a precarious moment.

Then awareness begins to expand again. But the rosy bliss of the Secondary Light is gone. Instead you find the undulating circumference about you is walled with mirrors—mirrors reflecting constantly changing scenes and forms. How very strange!—there you are, reflected in every one of the mirrors and surrounded by all the scenes and the forms. In every one of the scenes, you seem to be taking a vital part. Suddenly there seems to be a thousand mirror eyes, each one streaming thoughtforms and images toward you, and your reflection in each is constantly changing. The shifting scenes carry you through the drama of your entire life, and the *one* that was first reflected becomes a thousand strangers. Shadowy, impalpable forms, some assuming ghastly shapes, some changing from dark shadows to vivid colors, all merge toward you.

You are very apt to fear that you have gone to hell, and that fear is overwhelming. The foremost thought is escape. Unfamiliar with the Bardo journey, you imagine that you are being pursued by devils, unaware that the devils are the thoughtforms of your own past negative qualities—any greeds, lusts, hates, or selfishness. You are experiencing the lonesome valley of the Bardo—the third phase—the judgment.

The soul remains in this thoughtform valley of judgment while the entire "movie of memories" passes before your consciousness. You not only are viewing the scenes of the past, but you are taking part in them. It is a strange, almost weird, sensation to stand aside and watch yourself acting upon the stage of the life that has just ended. It is like watching a movie with yourself as the star.

Consider, for example, the biblical story of Jacob's battle with the mystical angel. The story is that Jacob grievously wronged his brother Esau. He took away Esau's birthright. He never sought forgiveness in any way whatever. One day he received a communication that Esau intended to visit him. This message filled him with apprehension because he feared Esau's intentions were to seek revenge and retribution.

The night before Esau arrived, Jacob had a dream. In that dream (a Bardo vision), there arose a man "with whom he wrestled," whose face appeared first as a manifestation of the face of God. Of course, since none of us knows what the face of God would look like, it is obvious Jacob was seeing a thoughtform of how he felt the face of God might be. Suddenly his opponent—the angel— manifested the face of Esau. In Jacob's dream, Esau assumed the form, power and face of an angel. His mind overwhelmed with guilt, Jacob demanded a blessing, or forgiveness. The angel granted the blessing. On waking and meeting Esau, a real forgiveness occurred.

The point here is that we build our own Bardo battles and the thoughtforms with which we wrestle—the dwellers on the threshold that we meet as we cross to the Otherside—are all symbols of our guilts, hatreds, greeds, jealousies, envies, and ego passions. These creatures are real only to the degree that we bestow force and power upon and within them, and guilt can indeed produce angelic qualities within those whom we have wronged. On the threshold of the Bardo, we meet the self-created thoughtforms of our enemies, our loved ones, and our worshipped deities. And on this threshold journey we face our judgment.

Every soul is its own judge. You know your own inner life better than anyone else, and are best qualified to judge — not what you do, but what you are. It is within your own personal conscience that the judge sits upon the judgment seat. We have been given the quality of judging ourselves and _that_ judgment speaks through the conscience. It is _this_ judge, pulling, pressing and urging from within, that forces you into a time of self-searching and self-realization.

It is the soul, itself, that is its own judge at the awesome judgment day when, held spellbound before a cosmic mirror, it is to read again the record of its past life on Earth. But even in the judgment, the soul is not dragged before some mighty monarch who casts the soul eternally into the fiery pits of hell or the golden streets of heaven. _You see yourself as you truly are._

The judgment, then, is the lower final stage of the Bardo, and is experienced only by the soul who failed to seek the light. This Bardo, then, is not a place or time of punishment dealt out by some cosmic judge, it is simply the enforced realization of the significance of the soul's own misdeeds, and it is the soul which will bear the burden of remorse and shame. (See figure 25 on page 92.) If you are unfamiliar with the Bardo, seeing these reflected images of yourself and not realizing what they are may cause you to flee in terror, seeking escape, not knowing that the pursuing forms personify your own thoughtforms.

Figure 24. Any judge sitting on a cosmic throne is only the thoughtform of such — produced by the misconception of religious teachings while you were on Earth.

You cannot escape them anymore than you could escape your shadow if you stood in the sun.

Remember, your body is lying asleep in a death trance, either for a brief time or perhaps a three-day period, undergoing a Bardo journey in consciousness. The Tibetans teach that it sometimes even requires a cycle of forty-nine "days" for the soul finally to "etch the atoms" which will create and release the new astral body. The forty-nine "days" the Tibetans refer to are symbolic of the forty-nine potential levels of consciousness that could keep erupting during this Bardo journey. Just as the seven "days" of creation do not mean seven actual days as we know time, but rather seven ages, or eons, or cycles of evolution, so the forty-nine "days" of the Bardo represent forty-nine erupting levels of consciousness.

Forty-nine is symbolic. Specifically, each of us has seven principles or bodies, each registering a certain level of consciousness. Each of those seven is subdivided by seven, which creates a total of forty-nine levels. These degrees of consciousness may be experienced within an hour's time or within a three day period. For the spiritual, the rebirth will be in the twinkling of an eye. But we're speaking now of the soul who, lying in a state of the Bardo sleep, is experiencing the judgment.

Remember this most vital point: during the Bardo, that which you desired most during life now becomes active. To repeat, it is during this stage that the emotional seed atom and the mental seed atom are attracting into the structure of the newly forming astral body the atoms which correspond to their own level of vibration. If the mind emphasized carnality and the emotions expressed only self-ish desires, they will attract into the new astral body the atomic particles harmonious with their own vibrations,

Figure 25. During the Bardo, you see yourself as you truly are—and the soul will bear the burden of remorse and shame.

and the newly forming astral body will pattern itself after this self-created thought image.

If the thoughts were beautiful and emotions unselfish, the soul's newly forming body will structure itself into a form of transcendental beauty. One is "reaping what he sowed."

The biblical scripture, "To him that hath it shall be given, and to him that hath not, even that which he hath shall be taken away from him" (Matthew 13:12), could possibly relate to this unique Bardo transition. To him that hath light, more light shall be given, at this propitious moment. To him that hath not light, even the small portion he may have unfolded could now be lost.

Let's consider one of humanity's greatest challenges — the lust of sex. If your thoughts focused principally on sex and the three lower chakras, then during the Bardo journey your soul will experience a lower form of energy rising up the spinal cord. The forms of the saviors, masters and deities will disappear to be replaced by different types of moving figures. Remember, you have not yet actually awakened to astral life. While undergoing the Bardo, you are still in the process of dying. You are in the labor of spiritual birth. Still on your Bardo trip, all this takes place in your consciousness while your body lies in an afterdeath trance.

It is a natural, biological process for kundalini to rise during this phase — but kundalini can also stimulate the sexual urge in those who focus most of their desires on the reproductive centers, the three lower chakras. The concept is: that which you most desired during life, or that upon which you focused your most concentrated attention, will now manifest.

Figure 26. *The spinning figures encountered during the third stage of the Bardo could produce a sexual urge and distract your consciousness from the Clear Light.*

So, if you constantly focused upon sex, a portion of kundalini may turn downward to stimulate the reproductive currents. As these creative energies attain full activity, the visions of the third Bardo state become filled with wavering, spinning forms (as shown in figure 26) which merge as if uniting for reproductive purposes. *The Tibetan Book of the Dead*[2] describes this phase as that just prior to actual human conception, and admonishes the pilgrim to "beware of seeking a womb door."

Actually these hallucinatory figures which dance, merge and spin together could produce a sexual interpretation in the mind of even the light seeker. You should recognize them simply as the result of the stimulated biological flow of creative forces within your new form and attach no personal interpretation to them or become involved in the visions. The enlightened pilgrim, experiencing the upsurging power of kundalini, will focus very little attention upon any biological sexual urge which may be aroused, because, since his thoughts were frequently focused upon prayer and meditation, he will center full attention upon the third eye chakras and the unfolding sense of intuitive illumination.

In the carnal minded, since the lower chakras occupied most of the attention, this soul may now allow itself to become involved in the sexual urge. Being unfamiliar with the rising of kundalini and the potential power now offered, this pilgrim is apt to be drawn into the maze of sexual activity. Such surrender to the carnal passion could possibly cause this soul to be drawn back toward a "womb door" and enter an immediate process of rebirth without even experiencing life on the higher planes at all. But this is rare.

_____

[2] *The Tibetan Book of the Dead* (London: Oxford University Press, 1927).

Usually the normal person will witness some degree of the Clear Light — perhaps not the first dawning, nor the Secondary Light — but will experience some portion of the light, awakening on one of the higher astral planes. Only those whose thoughts were filled with violence (murder, rape, etc.) will find themselves awakening on the lower planes, or experiencing an actual immediate return to rebirth.

Whichever the case may be, eventually the Bardo hypnotic trance comes to an end. The atoms are "etched" and the new astral body is formed according to your response during the Bardo journey.

With the completion of the Bardo journey, the heart seed atom departs and the silver cord breaks. When an infant is born, the doctor often grasps the tiny form by the ankles and, holding it head downward, slaps it over the lungs, encouraging an inhalation of breath and oxygen. With the snapping of the silver cord, there is an impact between the shoulder blades of the newly formed spirit body. The astral form inhales its first spirit breath, bringing awakening and awareness to life in spirit form. With the departure of the heart seed atom and the breaking of the silver cord, the actual moment or "time" of death occurs. When the life breath penetrates every atom of the new form, immediately the astral lungs inhale deeply, light sweeps over the entire form, transforming it into a reborn soul, either radiantly beautiful or displaying some defects, depending upon the quality of your thoughts and desires during life, and your Bardo reactions.

Now, should you have been a good soul, but the victim of some unwise habit, such as tobacco or intoxicating drink, your form will temporarily reflect the defects thereby created. You may temporarily be detained upon a lower plane, a plane of purgatory. But you are held there only until you can purify or purge your new form—not because you have been evil, but because you have been unwise.

Even when attempting to overcome the tobacco habit on the Earth plane, one goes through a period of "hell" while the body is being purified of the devastating effect of tobacco. The same is true of the astral form. One remains on the planes of purgatory only until the atoms and cells of the new form overcome the pull of the defects, or until the new form is purged or purified. One by one the cells that reflect the desire for tobacco or alcohol are sloughed off and gradually the astral form is purified, allowing the soul to depart purgatory to rise to more pleasant surroundings. The tobacco habit is evil only in that it has as devastating an effect upon the inner bodies as it does upon the physical.

It would be far better to overcome the tobacco or alcohol habit while still in the physical form. If not, should you, after death, waken on one of the planes of purgatory, remember that it is only temporary and, according to your own efforts, you will soon rise and find yourself able to bear the light of one of the higher planes. You will ascend as rapidly as you overcome, through the power of your will, your desire for the undesirable habit.

The same is not true of the person who is evil. The thought patterns of tobacco and alcohol habits affect only the individual, while the selfish and evil thoughts of greed or lust affect the whole wide world. Evil is reflected in the mind of those who scheme against their fellowman at every opportunity to attain their own purposes. Evil is a deliberate move away from God's will, with full awareness of selfish intent, usually with no thought of repentance, and no thought toward spiritual progression.

Many will waken on the planes of purgatory (an intermediary astral plane) to purify the new spirit body. The planes of purgatory do not relate to punishment, suffering being a result of the necessary purification—made necessary by the actions, habits, and thinking of the individual soul.

Chapter Five

THE ULTIMATE INITIATION

WE HAVE CONSIDERED the journey of the dark soul, the journey of judgment. But what of the light seeker—the initiate, the mystic? Let us now consider that you are such a soul and are approaching the transition called death. Your journey will be one of initiation into either the Clear Light or the Secondary Light of the Bardo. This happens when the main thrust of your incarnation (especially the latter part) was toward making the world a better place— seeking and sharing the light, displaying unselfish motives, learning to love, learning of the baptism of the Holy Spirit, awakening kundalini, opening the third eye, etc. Your rewards will now manifest.

As the actual death transitional period approaches, you will experience a gradual cessation of pain. You will experience a strange bouyancy pervading your body, and awareness of psychic faculties unfolding. If you have not been given consciousness-blocking drugs, then will come the phase of "balancing between the two worlds." You may rouse from the sleep of your terminal illness to see

Figure 27. During the phase of "balancing between two worlds," you feel yourself floating out of the confines of time into the boundless immensity of eternity.

those still on Earth sitting beside you, and also loved ones in spirit approaching from the Otherside. You may even rouse to say farewell to those on Earth, describing the loved ones who have come to escort you into the higher planes.

When this moment of balancing between the two worlds arrives, you will remember these mystical teachings for this is the great moment. All sense of physical pain and fear slips away and you feel only the sensation of being rocked on a resilient cloud. You may actually feel the departure from your loved ones while turning to those in spirit who have come for you. A sensation of "letting go" of your physical form may sweep over you. Earth loved ones will witness your collapse into the death coma, but you will be experiencing only a feeling of floating and freedom.

You may feel the entire sensorium expanding. Thoughts become increasingly vivid. You may hear and feel the snapping threads of the silver cord which are releasing you, much like an anchored balloon would be released from its moorings. As apprehension and fear fade away, you find yourself rising more and more into the light. All is love and all is right. You feel yourself floating out of the confines of time into the boundless immensity of eternity. (See figure 27.) You are drifting away from all things human, but you experience only a feeling of deep, sweet peace.

There is no grief, no sorrow—only great happiness. Limitations give way to expansion. An inflowing life force pervades your being. A glorious glow of colors transcends the surrounding mists. There's an ebb and flow of vibrant, flashing, dazzling radiance. You may feel that the Earth consciousness, which you are now departing, was indeed the dream or death consciousness, and death itself—the experience into which you are now passing—is an awakening to true reality. Such is the realization when kundalini becomes active.

As the physical world recedes, your consciousness melts into an ocean of boundless ether. Waves of unutterable love and exhaltation sweep over you as you diffuse like a breath into the bosom of infinite life and light. You are all and nothing. Every cell is being turned on with the light as your mind passes slowly out, out, out, to merge with the cosmic sea of being. You float on the fathomless deep, absorbing divine bliss, experiencing absolute reality. This is the moment for which you have waited. This is the moment for the approach of the Clear Light, the first stage of the Bardo, and your ultimate opportunity for initiation. This is the salvation offered you from the hand of God.

The Clear Light blazes before you, encompassing your being like water permeating a sponge. It becomes your breath. You feel yourself indrawing it as you melt into light, light, light!

For the light seeker, death is like sinking or rising into a blissful starlight. It is the outward ebbing of a tide. It is a glorious purple, crimson and gold dimming into an autumn sunset. Even to those trained to think in the reality of the afterlife, death comes as one unfolding surprise after another. Measureless, the light enfolds you, encompasses you, encircles you with lifegiving arms.

You realize that the drama called death is the very thing that makes life endurable. Death is the underlying spiritual impulse of the universe. Death is the living splendor behind the upgrowing springtime blossoms—behind the transmutation of all beautiful things.

The billowing clouds of light begin to stabilize about you. You become completely aware that you possess a body with head, hands, feet, but you feel as if you are total mind, all mind. Your new body is simply a light about you, but it isn't you. Only your mind is the total you and your mind embraces beyondness. If your mind could be described as substance, it would now appear to be soft, plastic, absorbent, like a mind-computer plugged into some vast cosmic stationhouse from which flows all the knowledge learned by your soul in all the countless past ages of lives, time and space. The barriers of crystallized Earth imagings, of space, structure and time, suddenly break and, like onrushing tidal waves, your mind computer absorbs the inpouring wisdom.

As your consciousness merges with the dazzling light, you become aware of the presence of angelic forms and of one special guide, whose quiet voice soothes away any fears as he or she points you toward ever higher lights.

Suddenly there bursts upon your awareness the most heavenly music you've ever heard, and you realize it is reaching you from the angelic lights as your guide bears you ever upward. As you soar into blissful regions of light, you are surrounded by a heavenly host bidding you welcome to their midst.

Then out of their midst emerges one solitary figure — the great Master at whose feet you have prayed and meditated while on Earth. And your guide whispers sweet words into your awareness. "This is your reward, disciple. Enter now into the joys of your Lord. Today, today shalt thou be with him in paradise."

For you — the mystical light seeker — there is no outer darkness, no Bardo, no lonesome valley of judgment. For many seekers, there is only the Clear Light, liberation and a waiting home in the regions of the blessed.

But for some the Secondary Light will be the way. If, during the first moments of death, the brilliance of the Clear Light transcends your ability to merge with it, it will fade away and be replaced by the Secondary Light. The first dawning of the Secondary Light enfolds you as the great silence, an infinite ocean of peace. Remembering death as the supreme initiation, you will be waiting for, and will immediately recognize, this Secondary Light. *This* is the light with which the majority of light seekers will merge.

The strange new sensation of superconscious awareness continues to break in upon you, crowding in like inflashing lightning, yet more swift. You feel like bursting into exuberant laughter at people's blindness, deafness, and dumbness—that we plod our weary way believing ourselves to be alive, when all the while true life and reality lie just beyond the confines of the body and the brain—here, where far-penetrating vision pierces the profound depths of space. From this supreme summit, with the radiant glory of the Secondary Light pervading your limitless perception, you survey the fields of eternity.

This is death? The question burns into your consciousness. This inexpressible bliss?—this unutterable joy?—this pure ecstasy?—*this* is death? Again there bubbles up laughter at the comedy we call life, merged with tears of agony that we suffer so in our unknowing.

How glad you are that you were a seeker of light! Never have your teachings and training about holding yourself surrounded by the pure white light been so important. You recall how you had taken the light affirmation so for granted when, all the while, there was a definite spiritual science underlying the teaching. How you wish you had meditated more, had practiced visualizing yourself surrounded by white light more. But even so, you seem to be doing very well indeed. From somewhere in the inner distant depths comes a memory: You remember words learned during years of seeking, when you attended services, classes, seminars, or read books such as this. A voice now reminds you:

"The reflections now before you, beloved pilgrim, are your own photographed thoughts. These are your own memories. Memory is nothing more than a photographic imprint of the soul. Everything you saw, felt, experienced in the world of matter engraved itself upon the plastic substance of your soul. But because you meditated, prayed or served often, because the burning desire of your life was to serve, to love, to unfold more light, now this perpetual, persistent desire becomes the measure of your reward. Such desire, as memories, now comes to life. When the analysis of your desires is completed, the new you will emerge bearing the total imprint of your soul."

From within the depths of the Secondary Light, there appears the thoughtform image of the one upon whom you meditated so often, the one to whom you most often prayed. The Western seeker, steeped in Christianity, will see the face and form of Jesus or the Blessed Virgin. The Jew may look to Moses. Devout seekers in Eastern cultures, feeling a closer attunement with Gautama Buddha, may see his form within this pure white light. The devout Hindu will seek aid from Siva, Vishnu, or Krishna. The Moslem will call for Mohammed.

Regardless which or whose form is seen—or even if the light is devoid of any form at all—it is this Secondary Light that the majority of light seekers will recognize, and

Figure 28. There is always one face more longed for than the rest, more loved, more missed. Sweet is a grief well ended.

it is the reflection of this light which transforms the consciousness.

You realize now the importance of meditating upon divine Beings during prayer times, for they rise at this moment as thoughtforms during the Bardo to form a magic circle of guidance and protection.

The light seeker faces no outer darkness. As your consciousness leaves the subjective state of the Bardo and comes into full wakefulness and awareness, the thoughtform images gradually merge into _the One_ upon whom you have actually meditated during life — the one to whom you have directly prayed. The happiest duty of such a teacher is to welcome seekers making the transition from Earth to spirit life. If you prayed often, even if you face some experiences in the lower phases of the third Bardo, you will never really be alone. Always this Master of the hierarchy will be standing by, waiting for the death trance to pass, when you waken to full consciousness. He or she will be waiting to greet you and ease away any fears or shock of your transition.

Let us say that, in your particular case, the Master Jesus is the one upon whom you focused most of your attention during meditation and prayers. He is the one now who welcomes your awakening, who escorts you in full consciousness through the beautiful planes on the way to your new home.

You pass breathtaking landscapes, magnificent cities, incomparable buildings, indescribable temples. Suddenly your eyes catch the light of a gleaming white edifice, glistening on a distant hilltop. You gaze at it in wonder and delight. "There, there," whispers the Master, "is your future home. There waiting for you are all you have loved and lost. Go, beloved, go." And you fly to the arms of loved ones waiting, and sweet indeed is your welcome among them. But there is always one face more longed for than the rest, more loved, more missed. This is the face you will now behold. (See figure 28 on page 106.)

How can my poor words describe the next scene? Only you can write the words. Only your heart can know what you will say, what you will do, how you will feel — only you and God.

Happy hereafter, beloved pilgrim and seeker of light.

Chapter Six

DEATH SATSANG

A _SATSANG_ IS a question-answer workshop which often follows a seminar. During the years I taught the death seminar, I invariably closed with a period of questions and answers. These sessions provided some very enlightening experiences and the answers given, channeled from minds far more enlightened than my own, offer teachings concerning death without which this book would not be complete. Following are some of the most intriguing questions and the startling answers gleaned from these sessions.

The Clear Light as the Holy Spirit

Question: During meditation, we strive to attain a union with God. You have said the Clear Light is like meeting God face-to-face. Could the Clear Light then be some aspect of the Holy Spirit? If we attain some measure of the

Holy Spirit baptism during life, would it act as a means of salvation during death?

Answer: I am constantly encouraged by my unseen teachers to speak more and more of the baptism of Holy Spirit and its effect upon not only our lives during incarnation, but also upon our souls in the afterlife. Thus my answer will surely be inspired by these very teachers, anxious to establish a greater understanding of the relationship between death and the power of Holy Spirit.

My memory flashes back to biblical days when, after Jesus ascended, the apostles and Mary the Mother met in the upper room to seek communication with the risen Master. On this auspicious occasion, there came upon all of them the pentecostal power of Holy Spirit. This baptism transformed each of them. Ordinary fishermen became teachers and extraordinary healers, going forth to spread the message of Christianity over their world. The Mother became their center of light and inspiration, acting henceforth as the channel through whom the ascended Master communicated instructions to further the future of the religion which ultimately became Christianity.

Their baptism and faith in the Holy spirit, then, transformed not only individuals but our entire planet. Jesus became, for millions, the Light of the World. He had much to say about the Holy Spirit. In fact, it was the Holy Spirit and its influence to which Jesus referred when he pointed to the comforter which he promised to send following his death. He explained that his disciples could not receive the comforter unless he went away. He said this comforter—as the Holy Spirit—would bring all things to their remembrance.

Such an experience, such as baptism, can open the awareness of the individual to a recall of the soul's true identity. Through such an awakening we become aware of the soul's past experience in previous lives. The soul, remembering the past, may be able to express talents suppressed until then. Such a baptism could even stimulate certain brain centers relating to talents developed by the soul in earlier life expressions. Is that why simple fishermen became enlightened scholars, philosophers, initiates, healers?

There can be no doubt that any measure of the downpouring grace of Holy Spirit aids the soul, not only during life, but during the death initiation and transition. The baptism of Holy Spirit and the awakening and resurrection of kundalini could be one and the same. The electromagnetic power of what we Westerners call the Holy Spirit, actually stirs kundalini to full arousal and draws it, through magnetic attraction, up the sushumna to the brain, where it unites with Holy Spirit and opens the third eye.

Defining Holy Spirit

Question: What exactly is the Holy Spirit?

Answer: If God could hold out a chalice to you filled with a potion of His divine love and explain that by drinking it you would be everafter saturated with that love — that would be the baptism of Holy Spirit.

The substance that flows through the universe, animating forms with the force called life, is a downpouring current from God. But it is not Holy Spirit. The mind force that flows into and permeates brain cells and seats of consciousness is a downpouring current from God. But it's not Holy Spirit either. The love force that flows through the universe stirring up love between human souls is a downpouring current from God — but it is not Holy Spirit. It *is* divine if it came from God. The divine love force that flows from the heart of God, filling souls with an overwhelming love and devotion to God — *that* is the Holy Spirit.

God answers our upreaching in various ways — and each of us responds according to the power to convey the love presence in our hearts. When the Holy Spirit baptized the disciples and the Holy Mother at the time of Pentecost, it came as the sound of mighty rushing wind. "There appeared unto them cloven tongues like as a fire, and it sat upon each of them." They were all filled with the Holy Ghost and began to speak with other tongues as the Spirit gave them utterance. "And many signs and wonders were done by the apostles."

Holy Spirit has only to do with the soul — your soul in relation with God's soul. Its purpose is to transform the soul into the actual substance of God's divine love, resulting in immortality for the human soul. "Except a man be born again, he cannot enter into the Kingdom of Heaven." Such an attainment, and such an entrance, is only possible through the purifying power of Holy Spirit, often called "the Comforter."

What has the Holy Spirit to do with death? Only that it can be received by the soul, whether in or out of the body. If it is received before death, it means liberation from karma. It so transmutes the soul, that soul becomes a light on earth, teaching, healing, leading and guiding others toward the same baptism and liberation. If received at death or after death, it means immediate ascension into heavenly planes, bypassing all the lower astral planes, and making the soul immortal.

Attaining the Baptism of Holy Spirit

Question: You seem to have experienced at least some measure of the baptism of Holy Spirit. Could you tell us how you, as an individual, brought that about? And could we, by following the same method, experience it?

Answer: First, let me say that I don't believe one "brings it about." One is "chosen" by God to receive it. It seems that, sometime during your life, the soul—through sorrow, grief, loneliness or pain—finds itself upreaching toward God with such fervent pleading that the light kindled by such a cry attracts the attention of the Heavenly Father and He, responding, fills the heart with such love that it opens to the inflow of Holy Spirit. It is the response of the Father in Heaven which brings it about—not the efforts of the seeker.

My own upreaching began as a child when, in sought-for moments of aloneness, I used to cry for a home I'd lost somewhere up among the stars. And other times of cosmic loneliness, when I felt the presence of a great spiritual Being who came from higher dimensions to soothe away fears caused by dogmatic preachers of hellfire and eternal damnation. But my real upreaching came through deep grief over the death of the pilot I had planned to marry. The airplane crash that took him into spirit also caused the crash of my own world as an actress—and I turned the full power of my grief toward prayer power, pleading that God would somehow let me pierce the veil that separated my world of matter from his world of spirit.

Once this prayer was answered, I continued to pray for divine love, for wisdom, for understanding, for illumination—for anything Godward. This prayer, too, was answered. Four different times during those bleak years, God reached down and touched my soul with an awakening that brought light and fulfillment to my seeking.

Thus I can't say *I* brought it about. I can only say that during the years of my quest, God responded most when I prayed, constantly, fervently, and in full faith that He *would* respond. My formula for assuring the baptism of Holy Spirit consists of constant prayer for the Holy Spirit from a heart filled with longing for God—not a prayer from the lips only. It should outflow in a stream of thought power so constant as never to be far from the consciousness. Regardless of your work, the thought of the prayer should underride your daily tasks so that throughout the day and night the upflowing thought current surfaces occasionally long enough for the lips to murmur a plea for response. Never should the prayer power be far from the conscious level of the mind and heart.

And sometime during the twenty-four hours of a day, time should be set aside for full attention to the outflowing prayer—either a time to meditate, to chant, to repeat your own rendition of the rosary or other prayers, or just to let the cry of the soul pour upward to the Father/Mother and the heavenly host of angels.

The prayer should be voiced in full faith that, sooner or later, God will respond. Each time a sincere prayer or meditation is projected, the light of the soul is enhanced. Such a lighted soul will ultimately warrant the down-pouring blessings of Holy Spirit, sent down by an all loving Father/Mother God.

Thus the two ingredients of my formula — that which has _always_ worked for me — are constant prayer and a full faith that the baptism would come. Even as I write, I must readily admit I have never experienced the Holy Spirit as I long to — one never does. No matter how glorious, how consuming is the baptism, the soul always cries for more. Indeed, fulfillment is the very thing that creates a hunger for more.

Ah, how empty seem the dreams of the Earth once the soul has "seen" the glories of the soul world, once the comforter has "brought all things to one's remembrance." Uppermost in awareness is the desire to unite again with that God-love, to feel again the ecstasy of the God-light which only constant prayer can bring.

After my experience with a vision of Mother Mary in the King's Chamber in the Great Pyramid of Egypt, I found my best prayer power through my own personal rendition of the rosary, the Lord's Prayer, the changed words of the Apostles' Creed, the Mercy Prayers, the Flame of Love rosary, or the Way of the Cross prayers. I changed the words and the procedure to suit my mystical trends, adding and changing various words, prayers, and passages from time to time to keep the power potent and not stagnant with automatic repetition.

I came to realize how powerful were the simple words of these various prayers when I was inspired by the Great Lady herself during a satsang following one of my seminars several years ago.

Figure 29. The rosary was superimposed by a powerful white light.

Someone had asked a question, "What can we do to protect ourselves during the times ahead?" As I prayed for a correct answer from my unseen teacher, suddenly I felt the entire room fill with a transcendent light. I knew a new and altogether divine Presence was in our midst as I "felt" words of instruction pour into my consciousness. I knew the great Lady of Light was near and speaking inwardly to me. Responding to her promptings, I reached for and held aloft my rosary saying, "This is your protection." At the moment I spoke these words, a photographer snapped a picture. (See figure 29.) When developed, the rosary was superimposed by a powerful white light. It could only mean that the reverential thought behind the words of the rosary, spoken daily and with a pure heart, could create an armor of light powerful enough to offer protection during any future negative happening.

The answer—given in the form of white light over a rosary—is too obvious to ignore. It answers all queries concerning prayer power far more explicitly than anything I could say. Because the armor of white light is unseen, the seeker must believe, believe, believe—and that gives birth to faith. Not a blind faith, but the faith that comes from trusting in a force that has never failed.

So again we turn to seeking the Holy Spirit. It is the only thing really worthy of attaining during the years of our exile here on earth. Should we not attain it—the longing for it—during the journey from birth to death, this life will have been lived partially in vain. We must return again and again, until we meet *the* life that finds the soul so hungry for God, no other love will do.

This brings us to a discussion of the true meaning of immortality. Once I thought immortality only meant that the soul goes on living after the physical death. That is only one phase of immortality. It seems to me, as I receive it from my Teachers, there are three aspects to immortality:

1) The truth that the soul lives on after physical death.

2) The truth that death does not actually confer immortality upon the soul. The soul seeks rebirth in a physical form again and again until such time as, having turned toward the light, it seeks union with God through the baptism of Holy Spirit—or, as many mystics refer to it, through the awakening of kundalini. Once the soul is filled with the divine love of Holy Spirit, only then does it become immortal, meaning that it need never return to a mortal form again. It has gained liberation from the wheel of life and death. It has burned all its karma. It can pass beyond the causal ring-pass-not and enter the Kingdom of God in the celestial realms of heaven. When the soul need no longer seek mortality—*that* is true immortality.

3) The third meaning is when the soul, having gained such immortality, chooses to return to mortal life as a teacher and possesses the power to persuade others to seek immortality for the mortal form.

Humankind has not yet evolved to the knowledge of immortalizing the physical form. Such a form would need to be consistently pure, the atoms vibrating at an accelerated voltage of electromagnetic power. Such a form would be capable of being transmuted into etheric and astral substance as the inhabiting soul dictated. The soul would be in total command of the sympathetic nervous system, controlling automatic functions and manipulating the form to suit the soul's mission on Earth.

Jesus possessed such a form. More than once he caused it to disappear when he was surrounded by his enemies. History may record such feats by other avatars. Appolonious of Tyana probably was another such teacher.

At any rate, this seems to be one status of future immortality—so that certain light bringers, having perfected a physical form, could at will transmute it into the substances of _all_ the planes and dwell on any vibratory level requiring their presence, from the physical to the celestial. But, again, such feats would not be possible until the soul had gained its purification and immortalization through the Holy Spirit initiation. Ultimately, this is the supreme attainment, and is that toward which all souls are tending—union with God through immersion in His own divine essence, the incomparable love of Holy Spirit.

There is another mystery connected with such immortality. When God first created his creature called man, this creature, this hu-man, dwelling on etheric planes, possessed an active share of the divine love and substance of the Heavenly Father. But when hu-mans, through disobedience to the divine laws, fell from their etheric state into the field of matter, they forfeited their connection with the divine essence of Holy Spirit.

Immortality of the soul—or liberation from the karmic wheel of life and death—was no longer possible. The soul must now incarnate again and again, slowly evolving toward such salvation.

When the race had evolved to its potential of being redeemed from such an unending cycle, the Father sent his first-saved Son, Jesus, to Earth to re-establish such grace. The incomparable teacher tried again and again to make his mission clear. He tried to tell his followers of the new birth, of being born again, of being saved from sins, being liberated from karma, of the possibility of being redeemed and never needing to be reborn on Earth again. Jesus tried to help them understand the new Law of God—that of redemption through love, through the baptism of a re-established Holy Spirit.

He tried to explain that the Father/Mother was offering the opportunity of salvation (or liberation) through the baptism of the Holy Spirit. That which hu-mans lost at the time of their Fall was now being offered again, for the birth of the "new man" (Jesus) had brought with it the essence of divine love, straight from the realms of light. Jesus tried to tell us the way to absorb the love essence (and be saved from future incarnations) was to pray and to love one another. Most of his listeners—even most of his disciples—failed to grasp the mystery.

It was only after his death, when the apostles and Mary were gathered in the upper room, that the down-pouring grace came. Everyone there, caught up in a moment of fervent prayer, was baptized with the divine essence of Holy Spirit. Such a baptism not only immortal-ized each soul, but transmuted the simple seekers into renowned teachers, healers and philosophers.

The message he came to impart—that our Father/ Mother God was re-establishing the opportunity for soul immortalization through the baptism of Holy Spirit—has not even yet been realized by the human race. His coming, his birth, his teachings, and his death, which brought with it the downpouring redeeming ethers of divine grace and the possibility of redemption from karma, have even now not been fully grasped. Someday we may understand.

Light can overcome darkness. Good can overcome evil. The darkness, the evil, and the karma of any soul— once it sincerely seeks redemption or cleansing—can be wiped out by immersion in the ethers of the white light. Again, the Master would have me say, "Seek to understand the true meaning of Jesus' sacrifice, the true meaning of the Holy Spirit: ultimate immortality." The Master would have you liberated from your karma so you may join the immortals in the realms of light following your death to never seek rebirth again.

How Does the Baptism Affect Death?

Question: You seem to lay great emphasis upon the importance of getting the baptism of the Holy Spirit. But what has that to do with death and dying? Does it affect one's death? Does the baptism assure that the soul will be "saved" and go to heaven? Or does it ensure that the soul need not incarnate again?

Answer: First, what has it to do with death and dying? It must be understood that receiving the baptism of Holy Spirit is imperative for salvation or liberation from one's karma, whether the soul is encased in a physical body or whether that soul is dwelling in the spirit life. The soul is still the soul whether in or out of the body.

If the baptism occurs before death, it certainly ensures that the soul will escape the Bardo journey to be raised to a high spiritual plane after death. If it occurs before, during or after death, it ensures liberation from karma or forgiveness for your sins.

There is something the seeker should understand. The soul _will_ continue to need rebirth in a physical body until that soul _does_ experience such a baptism. Without it, the soul may progress after death out of the hell planes and out of the darkness of purgatory, slowly working its way toward the planes of heaven. But once it reaches the causal plane, it cannot cross over that ring-pass-not until all karma connected with physical-matter expression is overcome. And the baptism of Holy Spirit is a signal that the summit has been met.

The soul can plod its weary way through evolutionary progression and, through many births and deaths, finally arrive at the moment when it has overcome all karma, and then experience the Holy Spirit baptism as its "certificate of graduation." Or it can turn to God the Father/Mother *now* in devout and constant pleading and prayer that sins be forgiven, until the Divine Parents, feeling the upreaching devotion of a seeking child, behold its anguish and sincerity and respond by pouring down upon that soul an essence of their own divinity through the holy baptism.

Whichever path the soul chooses, when the baptism occurs in full, the essence of the soul is transformed, actually changed. The downpouring grace brings with it a portion of divinity straight from the heart of God.

Once it enters the form inhabited by the soul, it stirs into awakening the dormant kundalini within. Such a happening actually transmutes the atoms of the spiritual body, and the creature made in the image of God becomes the born-again child made of the true essence of God Himself, partaking of His divinity. Until such a transformation occurs, the soul will seek rebirth in or on a field of matter, hungering after release.

Once this truth is fully realized, it behooves the soul to earnestly seek such a release, such a cleansing, such an awakening, such a baptism. This is why I so urgently point seekers toward the daily rosary or some other kind of daily prayer. The Lady of Light has promised fulfillment through the rosary.

Even as I speak, I can feel doubt arising, for someone is questioning, "How can repetition of the Hail Marys bring such a transformation?" The Master would have me say the following:

> The total auric forcefield is coded according to the light essence each soul has evolved. The genetic code in the RNA-DNA of our physical form will clearly reflect the encode of the soul, as it is recorded in each permanent heart seed atom.

> The living light of holy baptism can be drawn down through the sound vibration of holy names. The repeated sound waves break the "seal" of the genetic code. The sound of the names reconstructs the form of Adam-man into that of Adam Kadman. The sound current possesses all the key codes of super-specie creations, eventually changing the consciousness of biological limitations to correspond to increased chromosomal patterns—a recoding of the genetic chromosomes.

> Repeating the holy names establishes the energy of thoughtforms to be encoded into localized color codes, genetic codes, the heart seed atom.

> The constant chant of such holy names (acting as words of power in a magician's magical formula) creates a laser beam of white light with a specific wavelength which causes a chromosome to break its established pattern to be absorbed into the beam for genetic transfer to a new state of matter and an altered consciousness.

The seeker will be raising the genetic code of his or her life structure into a higher frequency code of consciousness by projecting it into and immersing it with a higher wavelength of white light. The human chromosomes are keyed to a low light-time zone. Repetition of sacred sounds—holy names—triggers the acceleration of the genetic code into the wavelength and reasonance of the Oversoul, gradually encoding the frequency of the white light time zone into and around the physical form.

So the repeated sound of holy names sets up a tone which gradually transforms your genetic code and builds a form of light. This can happen when the soul is incarnated or even after you ascend into spirit life. You can choose your own method of repeating the sacred sounds. You need not use the conventional rosary prayer. I frequently pray the Flame of Love rosary, visualizing the pillar of light which appeared on the astonishing picture when I held the rosary. Or I pray the Mercy Prayer rosary, or the Way of the Cross, the Credo (changed to my own wordings), the Lord's Prayer, the Hail, Holy Mother—all structured prayers containing the divine names, which keep my prayer hours vital and absorbing, preventing monotony through repetition.

What Does It Mean to Be Born Again?

Question: You mentioned that the soul will be born again through baptism experience. Can you explain just what is meant by being "born again"?

Answer: When the baptism of Holy Spirit encompasses the seeker, every atom and cell of every aspect of the soul is transmuted. The soul is encased in seven "bodies," all vibrating at various frequencies, each coded to a certain wavelength. When the God-essence pours into that force-field, the soul and all its sheaths experience a "new birth." Matter is simply matter until touched with true divinity. The God essence changes the voltage of the soul to a frequency that harmonizes with the universal void of the Godhead. The code barrier is broken and a new code established.

After that transmutation, the soul must maintain that frequency through prayer, meditation or service. If it does not, the high voltage will gradually slip away, and the atoms of the existing sheaths will revert to their previous frequency. Some of the light will be lost. If the soul maintains that light, when death comes it will merge with the God-voltage of the Clear Light. The light will carry the soul through the ring-pass-not of the causal plane, into the celestial planes where dwell the immortals—those who have also gained the baptism of Holy Spirit. The soul will have became immortal, that is, never subject to human birth again.

Only the baptism of Holy Spirit can give immortality to the mortal form, and only the souls dwelling on or beyond the causal plane have become immortal! All those who cannot pass beyond the causal are subject to rebirth on the physical plane.

This baptism of Holy Spirit was called initiation in the Mystery Schools of antiquity. The pathway of initiation included a rebirth for the candidate, who, after passing many tests, was placed in the granite sarcophagus in the King's Chamber of the Great Pyramid to enter a state of altered consciousness. During the ensuing out-of-body ceremonies, the soul submitted to baptism of Holy Spirit, and was thereby released from all animalistic tendencies. Such a release brought a new birth to the soul. The candidate awakened as an initiate, purified and "born again," emerging from the pyramid a Son of God, saved and immortalized.

When Jesus said, "Except a man be born again, he cannot enter the Kingdom of God," he was pointing the way toward the "born again" transmuting experience of Holy Spirit which awakens the dormant dynamo of kundalini and brings to birth the God power within. Until such a "second birth" has taken place the soul must seek rebirth on Earth (or another planet) until it realizes that to become immortal, it must seek a different kind of birth.

When the God essence of Holy Spirit permeates the atoms of the flesh form, they are transformed to divine atoms. The soul experiences an inner awakening and becomes a transformed being. The cells and atoms of the flesh form are now capable of being penetrated by a high voltage of Akashic essence which, until now, would have been too powerful to bear. As fermenting liquids will burst an unprepared container, so the vibrating essence of Holy Spirit would destroy an unprepared flesh form. When the fermenting power of Holy Spirit enters the flesh form, it continues a constant action of leavening, a slow or rapid transformation of "water into wine."

It should be understood that such a transformation can also occur in a spirit form. Thus if rebirth does not occur while the soul is incarnate in physical form, it can experience such a salvation in spirit form through constant prayer. There is no time or place where the soul cannot pray for and obtain the Father's divine love.

Hell and Purgatory

Question: You have touched upon hell and purgatory in that they are not eternal. Can you enlarge upon this?

Answer: Who can truly tell all there is to know about the lower realms of hell and the dark planes of purgatory! I can only share what I have received from my own teachers, and pray that my intuitive faculties have interpreted the information correctly.

First, about hell. I believe there certainly is a hell zone, contrary to what many new age teachers believe. I do not believe the soul is sentenced to hell eternally, nor do I believe in the hellfire so viciously described by fundamentalist Christian preachers.

What I believe is this: the planes of darkness lying so near the Earth life plane of matter were never established by God as a means of punishing His wicked children. Rather, it was created by the darksome thought essence of humankind itself. Since thoughtforce is real matter, and since energy follows thought, it concludes that the dark thoughtforce would, by natural affinity, accumulate in a field of expression, forming a zone inhabited by souls whose thought waves harmonize with the low frequency of the dark zone we have named hell.

Nor does God, through judgment, send souls to hell as punishment. The soul's own auric forcefield draws it into such an area through the law of magnetic attraction and affinity. The "fires" of hell, unlike the fires of Earth, are the fires of remorse. We have spoken of the mental reflecting ethers which photograph and make a record of every Earth happening. And we have said the drama of

Figure 30. Hell is witnessing the scenes of the soul's crimes until the soul, repentant, seeks to correct and compensate for causing suffering.

one's life flashes before the consciousness during the journey of the Bardo.

Well, to the soul in hell, the drama of the past life plays over and over again. The scenes of the soul's crimes unreel constantly before the memory vision. (See figure 30.) If you committed premeditated murder, you cannot escape the constant replay of the event, even to hearing the screams of your victim. Even though you may feel no remorse in the beginning of this hell experience, the perpetual "memory" of the deed, or deeds, eventually causes incomparable suffering.

Such haunting will relentlessly continue until you finally cry out for help from some source beyond yourself and such a cry is always answered. Some being of light will contact you. The succor given will relate to the degree of your repentance. Eventually you will be lifted into more comfortable zones—the zones of purgatory. You may remain there indefinitely, until, through prayer and penance, you purify your soul. Through prayer, repentance, and service to others to compensate for these destructive deeds the soul can gain deliverance from the zones of purification to abide in higher astral zones.

There are innumerable levels of purgatorial planes, some being only slightly shadowed with darkness. These will be temporarily occupied by souls caught in a habit difficult to overcome while in a physical form. They will remain on a fairly pleasant purgatorial plane only until the results of such a habit can be slowly eliminated from their new astral forms. Once the cells of the form are purified, the soul automatically ascends to higher planes of light, much like a soul on Earth entering an institution to go through pangs of withdrawal from smoking, alcohol or drugs.

The sufferings of withdrawal are very real, but the surroundings are comfortable. Help is forever forthcoming. The greatest suffering of souls in purgatory often happens because they are aware that some of their loved ones are in incredibly beautiful zones awaiting the time of their release. The separation is the greatest punishment. Thus I believe hell to be the "memory" zone of suffering and remorse for deeds committed while on Earth. Purgatory is the place of purification. Neither is eternal. When the soul in hell has faced his or her soul drama—the personal Book of Judgment—and realized within the extent of suffering he or she caused, the soul is allowed to progress gradually through higher planes. As you slowly purify your astral and mental bodies through prayer and service, so shall you progress through the astral and mental planes. On these planes, you will view, remember, and be compensated for any beautiful deeds or thoughts—just as you were punished in hell for wicked deeds and thoughts.

So shall we all ascend through the planes of afterlife—until we reach the causal plane. There we face the barrier of the ring-pass-not. We must return again to a mortal form and a field of matter to learn further soul lessons and to balance any debt of karma owed to those we wronged during previous lives on earth.

Remember, just because we were finally allowed to slowly ascend from hell doesn't mean we have leveled the karmic debt to those we wronged. It only means we have learned our own soul lessons through personal suffering and remorse. Such personal suffering does not mean we righted the wrongs done to other souls we caused to suffer. Return we must. Our return to rebirth is from the causal plane, the higher mental plane. The zones beyond this plane are far beyond the voltage of the soul's frequency.

We could never harmoniously dwell there. These higher planes beyond the causal plane are the homes of the immortals—the souls who have prayed for and received the baptism of Holy Spirit.

The only way a soul can prevent a return to rebirth, a return to a plane of matter, is to pray constantly for the baptism of Holy Spirit. If such prayers are sincere, if remorse is deep enough, if service to others is freely given, if we are truly repentant and ready for the light, the Father/Mother parent may decide to wipe out the karmic record, or forgive our sins, and allow entrance into the higher realms. We may warrant baptism of Holy Spirit. Once we gain access to these realms, we have gained immortality. We will never again be required to reincarnate in a form of matter.

Now some souls remain in hell a long, long time. They feel no remorse. They blame God for their suffering. So evil are they, the souls fuse with the "fires" of hell indefinitely—what would seem like eternity to us. That is the biblical meaning of "eternal hellfire." On the inner planes, there is no such thing as "time" as we know it on earth. Thus a long stay there would appear to Earthians to be "eternal."

If what I have just said is true, then it can clearly be seen that each of us holds the progress of our soul within our own keeping. It points once more to the importance of the Holy Spirit and the way to attain it.

Souls who seek baptism from the Father/Mother, and who attain to that forgiveness, have invoked the higher law of grace. Grace outweighs justice; it can purify the prayerful and repentant soul; it is a downpouring of divine love straight from the heart of God. No darkness can live therein. Once our hearts are filled with such love, whether in or out of the body, our hearts' seed atom is purified. Only that which is holy can dwell in hearts immersed in God's divine love, and only the heart so filled can become the Holy Grail, container of the Holy Spirit, the essence of God.

Since the hells and purgatorial zones were created by the thoughtforce of our own minds, it premises that the time will come when these lower planes will "pass away." As individual souls composing our human lifewave become evolved, one by one they will be liberated from their "sins." They will evolve into advanced stages of soul progression, learning the laws of compensation and love — learning also the value of white light thinking. They will cease to contribute darksome thought essence into the lower realms. Instead, they will graduate into and contribute toward the planes of light.

This can only mean the gradual dispersion of the hell planes and the darkness thereof. The inhabitants will become fewer and fewer as souls evolve into higher planes. The time will eventually come when all the souls of the lifewave will be "saved" and the lower zones purified and abolished — not by the workings of God's miracles but by our free will as we reach out for a return to the Father who created us.

How to Pray

Question: You consistently urge us to pray, but many of us don't really know how. I, for one. Once I've said, "God, give me the baptism of Holy Spirit," that's it. How do we pray, if we do not wish to say the structured Catholic prayers?

Answer: Nothing is so personal as prayer. I am reminded of what the Master said about it. He said pray not loudly on the street corners and churches, but seek your inner closet and pray in secret. He reminded us that the Father already knows our needs — He just wants us to ask. Asking is a form of sharing. Asking is a method of attuning your consciousness to spiritual levels.

Asking is also a demonstration of faith — faith in a power unseen — a source outside of and beyond us. We do not always need a ritualistic prayer because prayer begins in the heart. I remember, too, the Master said, "Pray without ceasing." Now what could he have meant? Having lived as a person here on Earth, he well knew the need for us to labor for our needs. So he knew we must devote much of our incarnation toward Earth's labor. Thus he must have meant that we should watch our thoughts.

We constantly think. There is hardly a time when we do not — except in some forms of meditation. Therefore we need to spiritualize our thoughts. Thinking pure love thoughts is a form of prayer. Once we know our only chance for "forgiveness from our sins," or liberation from our karma, depends upon our receiving the baptism of Holy Spirit, and once we realize we can't get the baptism until we fill our hearts with divine love, then we make an effort to practice human love to all people. Once we begin to practically practice love, we automatically begin to guard our thoughts. Once we begin to spiritualize our thoughts, our brain cells begin to be infused with a certain quality and condition — the quality of constant prayer.

Figure 31. You may prefer simply deep meditation. Silently repeat a mantram. Center your awareness on the third eye. Watch your breath. And love God with all your being.

To further light the brain and saturate the mind and heart with love, daily prayer is a must. I have already spoken of the need to chant sacred sounds to re-code the auric forcefield. Some prefer to simply hold the rosary in one's hands and talk to the Master and the Mother, occasionally saying a "Hail Mary." If you do not wish to speak structured prayers, then use them only as a pattern, a scaffolding upon which to form your own personal prayers. Or write your own daily prayers. But even when I choose to deviate from structured prayer, I always hold the rosary because it seems to be a tangible contact with the beautiful Lady of Light, the Blessed Mother.

Frequently, too, I focus my prayers upon the Master Jesus, using whatever words come into my heart and my mind. I do not think of him as God. I think of him as the highest endowed Son of God, possessing the greatest share of Holy Spirit, as the light of the world, and as my Master. Just as any disciple gives total obedience and reverence to his or her guru, so give I mine to this incomparable Master. I just talk to him. I voice whatever is in my heart. I ask for help and guidance in my undertakings. I offer my total being to service, and I voice my gratitude for blessings already received.

Sometimes I say the Stations of the Cross — the prayers of the Way of the Cross — which are totally to and for the Master. Again, you will need to change the words to embrace your own philosophy. Use them simply as guidelines. Keep the words of your prayers pure, powerful, sincere, and positive. You are a child of the light, a seeker on the path. Be very sure your prayers affirm that truth.

If the words of all rituals "turn you off," forget them. Instead of a rosary, hold your Egyptian ankh, your mala beads, your crystal, or whatever gem, stone, or amulet you prefer, and just talk to God. Ask Him directly for baptism. He hears. He always hears. And He always answers, sooner or later.

You may prefer simply to meditate — with no rosary, amulet or crystal. Just deep meditation. And this is one certain pathway to God. Meditate with your attention centered in the area of the third eye. (See figure 31 on page 134.) Silently repeat a mantram, or seek to bring your mental processes to a stillness, a deep inner stillness. If that is your preference, so be it. But be constant. Be steady. Be dedicated.

Whatever path or method of prayer you choose, be dedicated and be sincere. Whatever method you choose, the brain is being prepared for the downflowing power of white light. Receiving the baptism of Holy Spirit while yet in the body assures that your soul will meet the Clear Light face to face at the moment of death. Maintaining that light forcefield can bring you salvation, liberation and the highest initiation at the memorable moment of death.

The Resurrection

Question: I don't know if this has anything to do with death or dying — but I assume so. What is meant by the resurrection? What did Jesus mean when he said, "I am the Resurrection and the Life." Surely he meant more than just that we would live after death.

Answer: What I am receiving is rather startling, but I feel it must be taught, because apparently what the great Teacher meant by the Resurrection is totally different from that which Christianity presents. First I flash back to our beginning—let's say to the first race of souls represented by Adam and Eve before the Fall. These newborn souls, beginning their evolutionary journey as a lifewave on the beautiful planet Earth, were created with four principles:

1) _a physical body_ composed of the four higher physical ethers—light, pranic, akashic and mental reflecting ethers. The physical form was etheric and not clothed in the solids, liquids and gases which constitute dense matter;

2) _the soul_, which had not yet tasted of manifestation ensouled by a dense physical form;

3) _the spiritual form_, which overshadows every individual soul;

4) _the divine essence of the Father/Mother God_, a portion of its divinity, which gave the person the potential for aligning with God and becoming immortal—of never having to experience death as we know it in the dense physical body. This divine essence was an awakened kundalini, housed in the brain, which gave us an opened third eye.

Because of these active, awakened spiritual powers, the soul could evolve into its own individual divine godhood without ever needing to incarnate in the dense world of matter, without ever tasting death as we now know it.

When the first wave of souls disobeyed God's injunction, there came the Fall. It caused the lifewave to be required to depart the etheric realms and take on "coats of skin" in the world of dense matter. It caused the kundalini to fall to the root chakra at the base of the spine and become semi-dormant. It caused the loss of the potential of becoming one with God and gaining immortality. It caused the souls of the lifewave to "surely die," or to know death of the physical form.

The loss of the divine essence meant that the souls would need to evolve through a long period of incarnations in physical forms, unable to pass beyond the causal plane barrier to dwell in the planes of eternal life, or life without the necessity to incarnate again. For that is what eternal life truly means — life not subject to the death of the body.

As the millenniums passed, a few souls *did* gain immortality through Earth lives of total dedication to the love of the divine parents, but the Way was not accessible to the masses of the lifewave. With the coming of the Messiah Jesus, the potential for resurrection, or birth into eternal life, was restored.

Jesus never came solely to demonstrate life after death. Nor did He come to teach the resurrection of the physical form. He came to teach the re-establishment of the resurrection of the soul from the realm of the dead, or the world of dense matter. Revealing that the soul lives after death was a byproduct of the teachings of the Master. Such a resurrection of the soul, immediately after death, was always a part of our innate knowledge. The reappearance of Jesus after death only reinforced what we already knew.

As to the future resurrection of the physical form at some distant judgment or end-of-the-world time — why? When the soul continues to dwell in a spirit form similar, but far superior, to that physical form, what is the need or purpose for a resurrected physical form — a form composed of atoms of dense limitations? A principal purpose of death is to release the soul from such a prison.

And how? How can the atoms of a long-disintegrated physical form coalesce? As soon as the soul departs, the atoms begin their rapid departure to manifest in other forms. "Dust thou art to dust returneth," was not written of the soul, but rather was it written of the dense physical form. The atoms of this form are the "dust" of the physical plane, and this dust cannot be re-assembled for raising the same physical form. It would serve no cosmic purpose since the departed soul is clothed in a newer, better form. So what else could the Master have meant when He said, "I am the Resurrection and the Life"? He meant that His coming had restored to the lifewave of souls its lost potential for salvation, for liberation from the wheel of life and death, for resurrection into the planes of eternal life, from which the soul need "go no more out," need seek no more incarnations in the lower planes of matter.

"I am the Way, the Truth, and the Life," he said. "I have come to restore the potential of divine life to humankind. I have come to redeem people from their sins, to offer liberation from karma. Whosoever believeth in me shall never die. Follow the truths I teach and enter the higher celestial planes after death and never again return to an Earth subject to death."

The Master never meant that such a salvation was automatic. He _did_ mean that the potential for such a salvation was again available to every created soul. That soul must live a life harmonious to the laws of God while on Earth, must offer prayers of asking, must seek the light of divine love, must evidence a contrite heart for wrong doing, must sincerely long for union with God. Such seekers have the potential of merging with the Clear Light at the moment of death and "being saved" from ever having to enter again the land of "the dead"—the world of dense matter, the realm of darkness, the world of retributions, the plane of opposites.

I truly believe the principal mission of the Great One was as a Wayshower, that he brought to us from the Father and the Holy Ghost the incomparable gift of the true resurrection — that of eternal life; life in a land of no return. And we refer to this resurrection as the new birth — being born again, born of the spirit, indeed of the Holy Spirit.

When the soul is baptized in this divine essence of God, it is transformed. It is no longer just a creation of God, but a Son of God, being raised to a new and accelerated state of consciousness, awareness and perception. Such a soul is no longer simply made in the image of God — having life, intellect and the capacity to practice free will — but it now partakes of the Father's divine essence. Such a soul is "saved" in the true sense of the word, in a sense seldom understood by the orthodox Christian. Seldom understood by any, truly, except the saved soul itself.

The Law of Grace

Question: You have said that even though a soul, through remorse and suffering, finally progresses out of hell and purgatory, it still must reincarnate to level the debt of karma and right the wrongs committed against others. What about those whose sins are absolved through grace? Don't they still owe a karmic debt?

Answer: Let's first discuss those who suffered in hell and progressed. It is certainly true that hell need not be eternal. Even the most vile souls will eventually find that suffering is caused by their own dark forcefield, and remorse will prevail. They will be allowed to gradually progress out of darkness into lighter spheres.

But the fact that they suffered and experienced remorse does not in any measure compensate souls wronged during Earth incarnation. These souls—the sinners—must seek another Earth life. There they will inevitably meet again the same souls they wronged, and on the physical level, they must in some way serve the needs of the wronged until compensation for past abuse has been met.

Liberation or salvation from such a seemingly unending cycle is to seek for and obtain the downpouring blessing of Holy Spirit. Call it awakening the kundalini if you wish. Or call it opening the third eye, or attaining cosmic consciousness, or being "saved by grace." Such an attainment doesn't come without effort. It comes only to souls who seek the light. It comes only after devout meditation, prayer, or sincere longing for God. Such souls, aware that they must absolve karma, will make every effort toward living a life of love, service, and seeking.

When the baptism of Holy Spirit descends upon him or her, it means the law of grace has nullified the law of compensation. Grace, operating through the Holy Spirit, is God's divine law of forgiveness.

But, again, what of those souls who were wronged? Do we not need to still find some way to compensate them? Indeed, we do. From our home in celestial spheres, we must find ways to accomplish such service outside the law of requirement. We will not be required to reincarnate in order to meet this karmic indebtedness. Filled with the essence of God's divine love, from our abode in the celestial realms, we will find every opportunity to overshadow those to whom we owe a karmic debt, bringing unexpected blessings into their lives as they journey through incarnations on Earth. The law of love will override the law of necessity. This cosmic indebtedness must be paid to the last farthing, not because we must but because we want to. Only after this debt has been fulfilled will "saved" souls turn from Earth to seek wider Elysian fields of light.

There may be exceptions to this plan. If the higher forces have plans requiring the services of a saved soul that would prevent that soul from applying personal attention to alleviating old karma, then God Himself will see to it that the karmic debt is leveled. Such is the law of forgiveness. If God can forgive one soul its sins, or karma, He certainly can also overshadow and bless those deserving a blessing to whom the saved one still owes a karmic debt. One way or the other, the debits and credits of all concerned will balance. The scales of God's justice ultimately will find their cosmic balance.

● ● ●

Look to the light, Seeker! Look to death as life's highest adventure. Look to death as the soul's greatest hope for initiation—the soul's ultimate union with God. So live that when that moment of opportunity approaches, the portals of paradise will open wide and a voice from the Clear Light will bid you entrance:

"Well done, good and faithful servant. Enter now into the joys of eternal life."

INDEX